T0311273

HOMO CONTRIBUENS
THE NEED TO GIVE AND THE SEARCH FOR FULFILMENT

Homo Contribuens

THE NEED TO GIVE AND THE
SEARCH FOR FULFILMENT

☙

Hisao Taki

RENAISSANCE BOOKS

FOLKESTONE, KENT

HOMO CONTRIBUENS
THE NEED TO GIVE AND THE SEARCH FOR FULFILMENT
By Hisao Taki

Japanese edition, *Koken suru Kimochi*,
first published 2001 by
Kinokuniya Company Ltd., Tokyo

First published in English 2008 by
Renaissance Books

*Renaissance Books is an imprint of
Global Books Ltd
PO Box 219
Folkestone
Kent CT20 2WP, UK*

www.globaloriental.co.uk

ISBN 978-1-898823-65-0

British Library Cataloguing in Publication Data
A CIP catalogue entry for this book is available
from the British Library

Set in Garamond 12 on 14pt by Servis Filmsetting Ltd, Manchester
Printed and bound in England by Cromwell Press Ltd, Trowbridge, Wilts

CONTENTS

☙

Contents

For my wife, Hiroko

PREFACE TO THE ENGLISH EDITION

❧

In this book I elaborate the notion of the urge to contribute as it relates to the dynamics of self and other and to contemporary society as constituted by various self-other interrelationships.

I am no professional philosopher; my career has been devoted to the business of transportation advertising and to an enterprise that applies information technology to enhance food culture. But my interest in philosophical questions is nonetheless deep-seated and long-standing. It springs from two pivotal moments in my life. The first occurred when I was in junior high school and learned that my friend's older brother had developed a terminal medical condition. I was deeply moved by the way that young man took the prospect of his own imminent death as an opportunity to live what remained of his life with great vigour and purpose. The second moment came years later when, not long after I had established my business, I myself was diagnosed with a malignant form of bone cancer. At first glance, the idea may seem trivial. How could simply thinking of the urge to contribute as instinctual hold such potential for improving our lives? The answer lies in how this view differs from the usual understanding of altruistic behaviour. In conventional ethical thinking formulated along the lines of the categorical imperative, the urge to contribute is seen as a learned or acquired 'virtue'. But when considered instead as an instinct, our urge to act in the interests of others becomes no more worthy of either praise or censure than our hunger, our sex drive, or any of our other instinctive desires and compulsions. This understanding of the desire to be useful as a natural, innate part of being human, essentially neither good nor bad, is the catalyst for a whole new outlook on life.

Under the impact of these personal experiences, I found intellectual guidance first of all in the philosophy of Socrates and later in the writings of Shakespeare, which opened my eyes to many key elements of human nature. Having been born in Japan, I was very fortunate to be able to draw on both Western and Eastern thought and sensibilities in these intellectual explorations. This is evident in this book, in which (at the risk, perhaps, of a certain amount of misunderstanding) I offer my frank interpretations, not only of aspects of Western philosophy and the Western view of humanity, but also about the culture and outlook on humanity, typical of Japanese and other Asians – though this is not in any way intended as an opportunity for passing judgement on which view is right or wrong.

The twenty-first century has been called the century of the global family of humanity. It is envisioned that the diverse peoples of the world will achieve greater understanding and acceptance of each other's cultural, historical and religious backgrounds; that all people will thereby connect with one another more securely at the level of their common humanity; and that in this way we will achieve peace and well-being as a truly global family. I believe that the key to that common connection is recognition of the urge to contribute as a human instinct, and I have no doubt that this recognition would inspire people to play their part in striving for a better world as members of the global community of Homo contribuens.

Finally, for the benefit of my ongoing exploration of the ideas presented in this book, I would welcome readers' frank responses to it and comments on the central theme. Interested readers are invited to write to me care of the publisher.

Hisao Taki

FOREWORD

By

IKUO HIRAYAMA*

☙

It is my great pleasure to contribute to this publication of the English edition of *Koken suru Kimochi (Homo Contribuens)*, originally written in Japanese by my longstanding friend Hisao Taki, a graduate of the School of Engineering, Tokyo Institute of Technology. Taki heads a number of successful transit-advertising and IT-related enterprises. Among his achievements is the creation of the restaurant search site Gourmet Navigator Inc. This company, founded more than a decade ago, expanded rapidly and in May 2005 was listed on the stock exchange.

Taki has long been engaged in a wide variety of cultural activities contributing to the enrichment of society. He has used his status as a successful entrepreneur to provide scholarships for students at art schools overseas, as well as providing financial support for children of people employed in transportation-related businesses. He serves on the board of directors of the

---

* Japanese-style painter. He is former president of the Tokyo National University of Fine Arts and Music, UNESCO Goodwill Ambassador, chairman of the Foundation for Cultural Heritage and Art Research, president of the Japan Institute of Fine Arts, adviser to the National Institutes for Cultural Heritage, and chairman of the Japan-China Friendship Association, among other posts. His many honours include the Order of Cultural Merit of the Japanese government (1998) and the Légion d'Honneur of the French government (1995).

Foundation for Cultural Heritage and Art Research of which I chair. Even this brief profile does not do full justice to Taki's diverse commitments. In addition to his involvement in business and social activities, he is deeply immersed in philosophy.

The essence of Taki's philosophy is that man's aspiration to do something for others and contribute to society arises, not merely from a sense of duty or a need for self-sacrifice, but from an inborn and intuitive urge.

Koken suru Kimochi is cited in Japan's authoritative encyclopaedia of philosophy and ethics, *Gendai Rinrigaku Jiten* (Kobundo, 2006). In this sense, *Homo Contribuens* – man the contributor – the term Taki coined and explores in this book – is becoming part of accepted parlance in the field of philosophy and ethics education. At the Tohoku University of Community Service and Science, *Koken suru Kimochi* is used as a class text and an excerpt from the book was also used in the testing of reading comprehension in a university entrance examination.

The Homo Contribuens Research Institute was founded in 2003. Led by eminent scholars such as Hisatake Kato, professor emeritus of Kyoto University (former president of the Philosophical Association of Japan), Masuo Aizawa, president of the Tokyo Institute of Technology (specialist in life science and technology) and Yasuaki Nara, former chancellor of Komazawa University (scholar of Buddhism), the institute's activities recently entered their fourth year. I, in accord with these scholars, am a firm supporter of the views posited in this book.

Taki's philosophy and ideas about the human urge to contribute have received widespread acceptance. Shoji Sumita, principal executive adviser of the East Japan Railway Company, praised the work as 'a textbook of ethics and philosophy for our times', describing Taki's propositions as a philosophy that 'elucidates how working for others or contributing to society is ultimately a practical way of doing something for oneself'. I agree, and we are imbued with a sense of fulfilment and peace of mind through contributing to the welfare of others. In the course of expressing the urge to contribute horizons are widened and the future enhanced.

One of the reports submitted in the seminars of the Homo Contribuens Research Institute introduced the experience of Hiroshi Tomita, executive director of a non-profit organization called the Japan Alliance for Humanitarian Mine Clearance Support. Needless to say, mine clearance is a high-risk occupation, and Tomita initially experienced great fear, physically and psychologically, while working as a volunteer in mine clearance operations in Cambodia and other parts of Asia. He happened to see an advertisement for *Koken suru kimochi*, and subsequently purchased it. Reading Taki's book led Tomita to the realization that his voluntary mine clearance work was a self-serving undertaking and this revelation alleviated all his feelings of worry and fear.

As Taki explains in this book, human beings are referred to as *Homo sapiens* ('man the reasoner') in biology, but also *Homo faber* ('man the maker'), the former focusing on man's capacity to think and learn and the latter on man's ability to produce things. He argues, however, that above all human beings are *Homo contribuens* ('man the contributor') who, by their nature, are impelled to contribute to a better world.

I, too, am among those who seek to contribute to society, and as a painter I have engaged in the international activities of such organizations as the Foundation for Cultural Heritage and Art Research and UNESCO. When I heard of the pending publication of the English edition of Taki's book, I was eager to add my voice in recommending it to readers. The book illuminates the intuitive urge to contribute, an urge that lies dormant within us but of which we are often unaware.

The English edition was prepared by Hiroko Taki, specialist in the works of nineteenth-century English novelist Charles Dickens and wife of Hisao Taki.

April 2007

HOMO CONTRIBUENS

ℭℛ

Unlike most highly regarded books by authors who are also men of business, *Homo Contribuens* is unique in tracing industrialist Hisao Taki's personal journey of philosophical and ethical development. The reader is asked to return with him to his lifelong quest: Is the Urge to Contribute an instinct rooted in the human heart? And if so to what extent can we activate this urge?

In his examination of the Japanese or Asian way of thinking, '*mono no aware*' (literally the pathos of things) and 'being enabled to live' by the grace and effort of others, Hisao Taki convinces us that the urge to contribute is a basic and universal instinct which enables us to find the way towards a healthy and happy personal life leading to a comfortable and enriched society. He also exemplifies good practice of the urge to contribute in his own business successes, fusing Japanese dining culture with information technology as well as weaving art and information technology into traffic culture. It is fascinating that his business methods have embraced the aim of serving others and contributing to society.

Homo Contribuens

This is a stimulating read about how we think and how we solve seemingly impossible problems of corporate, social and personal life by exercising the instinctive urge to contribute.

Masuo Aizawa
President, Tokyo Institute of Technology
Executive Member, Council for Science and Technology Policy
Cabinet Office, Japan

PREFACE TO THE JAPANESE EDITION

CR

In a relentlessly complex world, societies and lifestyles are perpetually changing. Even the limited constellation of elements that impinges on any individual life teems with diversity and continually revolves around us, opaque and perplexing. Many people feel an indefinable deficiency in coming to terms with today's world, which could perhaps be alleviated by divining an immutable essence of human nature through which we could gain an understanding of the world and our place in it. Yet even while we recognize the need for a new philosophy, we are reluctant to embark on a serious intellectual quest for solutions as past experience has shown that both personal and social lives remain less complicated when unencumbered by searching questions. To immerse ourselves in a labyrinth of philosophical contemplation is indeed a risk, but while it may be possible to avoid life's important questions by suspending thought, a certain disquiet tells us that something is lacking in the way we live and in our relations with others. Perhaps we see no clear direction for ourselves, feeling a lack of centredness in our existence, and in the absence of some kind of inspiration it is very difficult to rise above this slough of uncertainty.

There is a way of thinking, however, that clarifies and helps to resolve some of the complex yet crucial questions in our lives; its nucleus is the belief that people are born with an altruistic instinct, a compulsion to do something for the world, an urge to contribute to society.

In geometry, sometimes an auxiliary line is drawn as an aid to solving a problem. The urge to contribute can be perceived as a kind of 'auxiliary line' that helps us live fuller lives in today's world. It is a perception that can serve as a signpost showing us what course in life to take when we are irresolute. At the same time it can serve as a central indicator helping to guide society as a whole.

If we recognize the urge to contribute as a universal, basic instinct, such an understanding can reveal the way to achieve healthy and happy lives for individuals, as well as a more content and enriched society benefitting from a range of salutary effects. In simple terms, the contributing instinct could, for example, help control teasing and bullying among children, or crime and delinquency among teenagers, and in adults incidents of uncontrolled rage, or the deadly activities of subversive cults like Aum Shinrikyo.

How, you may ask, could the 'urge to contribute' have such a positive effect on our lives? What difference does it make whether we understand an altruistic spirit as an instinctive urge or an obligation dictated by culture and society? The conventional view of people who make efforts to contribute to the well-being of others is to classify them as virtuous and socially responsible, qualities that are taught and learned. If, on the other hand, we recognize the desire to help, to give, *to contribute* as a natural human instinct, we see that acting in the interest of others is neither exceptional nor worthy of special praise. It is no more or less than hunger, sexual appetite, or any other natural urge. It is inherent in our makeup, neither bad nor good but indisputable. What is important is to recognize that we all have an inner need to make ourselves useful, and that need is an innate, natural force in being human. That recognition promotes a whole new outlook on life; a new philosophy begins to take shape.

The fusion of the two seemingly unrelated concepts, the urge to contribute and natural instinct, gives rise to an intellectual force that allows a new way of thinking and gives a fresh perspective on human beings, society and corporate activities. Coincidentally, the principles underlying the new concept can be a catalyst that invigorates individual life at home, at work and social life in all its aspects.

The term instinct as used in psychology usually refers to inborn urges and desires towards typical patterns of behaviour. Instincts are understood as responses or inclinations, sometimes subconscious, that are genetically programmed, not as aspects of intellect acquired through training and education. The influential American psychologist A. H. Maslow (1908–70), for example, posited that instinct-driven human desires are basic physiological responses controlling our most primitive urges.

Just as commonly, to contribute something to the world is regarded as a means to realize the noblest aspects of human intellect. From this point of view, it is an aspect of human nature that arises from a spiritually elevated, purposeful desire for self-sacrifice, and it becomes assertive when we consciously direct feelings of love and concern outwards, towards the people, society, culture or environment that surround us.

What I propose here, however, is to consider the urge to serve others as something instilled in us by nature, deriving not from the intellect but from instinct and expressed naturally. I see it, in other words, as an innate (*a priori*) drive rather than a learned (*a posteriori*) response.

This hypothesis points towards a new understanding of human beings. My term for this new conception humans is *Homo contribuens*, which I will discuss more fully in the section in Chapter 2 entitled 'The Fifth "Life Mode" '. To summarize my argument, the urge to contribute is given expression in the same way as our physiological urges for food or sex. Arising spontaneously, it is not motivated by any moral consciousness or sense of virtue, but stands among the other natural urges we strive to gratify in order to attain health, normality and balance.

Three major elements that figure in my concept of *Homo contribuens* are the self, the other and contemporary society as constituted by the self and the other. Chapter 1 begins with an event that ignited my lifelong engagement in philosophical inquiry. Drawing connections between that personal experience and the development of classical Greek philosophy, I show how the principles that underlie the urge to contribute were recognized even by ancient Greek minds. In Chapter 2, I present the new perspective that emerges when we acknowledge the urge to contribute as an instinct, and I show how this approach can be applied to one's own life. In the remaining chapters I take this perspective, with liberal use of familiar examples, to analyse the self, the other and contemporary society in order to accomplish a twofold objective: to identify in broad terms where our era is headed, and to sketch a new vision of humanity, society in general and corporate life.

LIST OF ILLUSTRATIONS

☙

Illustrations by Eibin Otsu

CHAPTER 1

AN EARLY PHILOSOPHICAL EXPERIENCE AND A JOURNEY BACK TO ANCIENT GREECE

ଓ

The importance of some experiences can escape us
if we let them pass without much thought.
We might realize someday that they contain a hint,
like an auxiliary line in geometry,
on ways to solve problems in our lives.

Memento Mori

My first encounter with a philosophical problem was long ago. Since then my focus has changed, but that event provided the germ of my later enquiry into what I call the 'urge to contribute'. The event that kindled my interest took place during junior high school. At that time, when I was in my second year, the older brother of a close friend died. His death was tragic, but the real, soul-stirring impact on me came from learning how this young man (I will call him Takeshi), still only a high school student, spent the remaining few months of his life after being diagnosed with terminal cancer.

For a while after he was told of his condition, and quite out of

1

character, Takeshi surrendered himself to hedonistic pursuits. But about three months before he died, he pulled himself together, rejected frivolous distractions and resumed his studies. In the brief time left to him Takeshi tried to complete the academic work he had left unfinished.

Even now I can only wonder how this boy, still in his teens, was able to deal with the looming shadow of death. But he alone made the decision to devote the remainder of his tragically shortened life to the quiet pursuit of learning. To me, though I was still in junior high school, there was a depth of meaning in what he did. It seemed to challenge understanding, and opened my mind to complex issues. In that sense it was my first experience of dealing with philosophical ideas.

Throughout history, across cultures, in disciplines ranging from biology and medicine to philosophy and religion, death has been an ever-present theme. All of us have to face the death of someone we know at some time in our lives, and eventually our own. One prevailing attitude to death in medieval Europe was encapsulated in the Latin reminder of our mortality, 'memento mori' ('remember that thou, too, must die'), echoes of which have come down to us in scholarly writings of those times, symbols in art and Christian practices up to the late 1700s. During the late Middle Ages in Europe, thoughts about death proliferated and grew more complex; death became something more than the occasion of a funereal rite. Those ideas helped build the foundation for a European view of life and death that developed through the Renaissance and has persisted in some form or another to the present day.

People spent their lives trying to perfect the 'art of dying'. Anyone on the brink of death, even were he counted among one's enemies, was still part of the wide human corpus and was regarded as a pioneer going forth into a great unknown where all would one day follow. His every gesture, every move, was seized upon as prophetic. Vigilant observers drew numerous and varied lessons from the smallest incidentals of a death. The words and actions of the dying person were carefully marked and passed down, to become instructive lore for future generations.

Another layer in my first brush with philosophical thoughts may have been shaped by questions about *memento mori* and the inevitability of death, questions stimulated by the way Takeshi responded as his own hovered near. What made him turn to study at that critical juncture? That question planted in me a new sense, albeit a vague one, of meaning in human life. Takeshi's first reaction might have been nihilism, an angry lament that no matter how diligently one strives in life, it all comes to nothing because in the end we die. But would a teenage boy, advised that he was terminally ill and would soon die, plunge into serious study if he had succumbed to nihilism? It seemed to me that had Takeshi descended into such a psychological state, he would hardly have decided to spend his last months immersed in books. Usually nihilism leads to decadence. Maybe something like that impelled him towards the initial pleasure-seeking when he learned of the diagnosis, but nihilism could not explain his transposition to diligent study.

As I struggled to understand, I had a sudden insight into the nature of Takeshi's reversion, what really lay behind his resolve to halt the hedonism and resume studying. Ultimately, I now saw, he had drawn on a sense that all people are born with. Up to this point Takeshi's immersion in study had struck me as meaningless, but as I thought about it in this new light, his final quest was transformed in my mind into a noble and dignified struggle. The image of this boy, quietly proceeding with his studies while confronting life's ultimate crisis, struck me as epitomizing some essence, some essential quality in being human. But what quality was that?

In retrospect, what troubled me about the cessation of life was not how people overcame the fear of inevitable death or the profound resignation that fear tends to evoke; it was not the matter of accepting death. In terminal cases, flight into hedonism is often part of the process of accepting death. It can be understood as one way for the dying person to cope with the anguish of imminent death by living life to the full in the time that remains.

When I saw a doomed young man reject such diversions and immerse himself instead in study to the very last, heedless of physical pain and mental anguish, I was stunned. That determination was to me a poignant expression of a human quality discrete from any medical interpretation of death. I perceived it as something that could be explained only through philosophy.

So it was questions about death that inclined me towards philosophy. Anyone who has not faced imminent death does not have the experience to knowledgeably propound about the psychological process of dying. That people die is, after all, merely another law of nature. What changed everything for me was the fact that Takeshi was close, the brother of my friend. He was going to die and I witnessed firsthand how he faced death. From that I derived a life-changing insight into the nature of the human heart.

Recent discourse on life and death leaves me unsatisfied. Before any talk about terminal care or medical options, people need to learn about death and how to prepare for it. Society also should have a role in empowering people with that understanding, the foundation for which is philosophy, where the essence of the anguished and reflective human being makes its most unambiguous statement.

Socratic Irony

We have not solved any of the great mysteries of nature and life, but we still live our lives perfectly well, moved by our human instincts. Yet towards the end of our own life, or perhaps when we bid a final farewell to a loved one, it is natural to reflect on how we have lived our life. At those moments when we realize that we

Sketch of Socrates

– based on a Roman-period replica of a sculpted bust of Socrates.
Known as the father of Western philosophy, Socrates regarded
'awareness of one's ignorance' as the rational thinker's starting point.

have no ready answers to life's critical questions, we can choose to respond in a number of ways.

One option is to conclude that there are no definitive answers to the major questions of life, human existence and so on. Many people of this opinion think we should not even consider such questions. This is scepticism, a philosophical position that doubts our ability to know the world. An alternative is to seek answers using reason, which is the rationalist approach. At this point it might help to take a closer look at scepticism and rationalism through the lens of ancient Greek philosophers in order to construct a framework for exploring the question that formed in my mind as a result of my boyhood encounter with the death of Takeshi: what is the essence, the unchanging core, of human nature?

The sophists were a group of professional teachers who were active in Athens and other city-states of Greece around 450 BC. They included many sceptics, thinkers who believed it impossible to discover any ultimate or absolute truth. Sophists were among the first to openly question the substance of traditional Greek myths and consider the possibility of them being simply human fabrications. Through this, and also by elevating the arts of rhetoric and oratory to new levels, the sophists pioneered pathways in Greek intellectual history.

On the other hand, following their sceptical leanings, the sophists believed that no man could ever find definitive solutions to the fundamental mysteries of life and nature. As teachers they travelled widely and were able to observe how moral principles, ways of thinking and global concepts differed from place to place. Gaining a sense of the relativity of perceptions, they concluded that reality is only what people take it to be, or, in the well-known words of Protagoras, 'Man is the measure of all things'. This refutation of a single, universal truth, transcending vacillating human perceptions and beliefs, was a declaration that the nature of things metamorphosises according to ways of thinking.

Rejecting philosophical discourse about the ultimate reality of things, the sophists denied the existence of universal criteria of right and wrong. A corollary was the sophist premise that people can express their particular *doxa* (viewpoint) only in their own terms, conforming to their own standards–hence the sophist emphasis on knowledge of law and politics and skill in rhetoric and oratory aimed at persuading other individuals and society as a whole to accept given views. Sophist teachers put these ideas into practice by studying the character of selected people or communities and coaching students in employing techniques of persuasion (rhetoric) to best effect in each particular context.

Then in the first part of the fifth century BC there appeared a formidable figure who challenged scepticism and sophism head-on with the proposition, based on rationalism, that there is an ultimate, unchanging reality that is always true at any time, in any place, whether or not it is divined. I speak, of course, of Socrates. He spent much of his life in the market place of Athens questioning, examining, arguing – hence his nickname, the 'gadfly of Athens' – refining ideas on ethics, truth and virtue, and the philosophical methods that have had such a profound and enduring impact on European thought.

Socrates argued that by reasoning we are enabled to grasp that which is true, the essence of things. This includes the truth about ourselves: what is essential in human nature is not subject to individual value judgement and is accessible to us, but only through rational inquiry and contemplation. By rationality, Socrates meant using one's mind to think through a problem to its logical conclusion, or using a process of reasoning to examine even the most difficult questions.

Socrates differed in fundamental ways from the sophists, not only in the substance of his ideas but also in practice. He did not believe that the techniques of persuasion could ever lead to real understanding. Also, he contended, on many questions it is impossible to convince others of your views, no matter how cogently you present them. He took a different approach, the account of which comes down to us in the works of his most famous student, Plato.

As he is portrayed by Plato, Socrates maintains that unless we apply our own powers of reason to perceive the essence of a thing, we can never truly understand it. We can attain true knowledge only through the exercise of reason.

Socrates' method can be described as 'non-persuasion'. He practised it by spending his days in the public forums of Athens, engaging young men from aristocratic families and others in dialogue that resembled cross-examination. Wishing instruction on a topic, he placed himself in the role of the who, putting questions to another. No matter how contradictory his interlocutor's statements, Socrates never curtailed an argument with impatient criticism of the error, but guided the discourse through a combination of carefully crafted questions and attention to the answers until the incongruities in reasoning made it all too obvious that the original assertion was invalid.

The Socratic dialogues follow a typical pattern: the interlocutor continues speaking until his points are made, oblivious to flaws or inconsistencies. As the argument develops, he finds himself finally unable to continue, at a loss for direction, mired in wondering confusion (*aporia*). Clearly something is not right – the answer is not, after all, self-evident. Socrates interjects then to expose the fallacy in reasoning, revealing how assumptions about life's questions can be deceptive. By guiding his students to see the pitfalls in their arguments, Socrates helps them to apply reason, as far as they are able, to get closer to the truth of the question.

True understanding is achieved solely by the mind, by the thinking subject heeding the inner voice of reason. We always have a choice: to let ourselves be persuaded by someone else's view, or exercise our own reason. But there is a fundamental difference in the kind of understanding that is achieved, the first is passive, the second active. For Socrates, who took reason to be

8

the only means of knowing the true nature of human beings, it was inconceivable that genuine knowledge could ever be assimilated by something external like the techniques of persuasion. If the arguments his pupils made contained fallacies or inconsistencies, they would never understand those errors until they deduced for themselves.

The method Socrates practised was thus based on a dialectic process in which he never categorically exposed, denounced or corrected the errors in others' pronouncements. In posing his questions, he would humbly profess ignorance and the desire to be enlightened. In philosophy this intentionally unassuming approach in the search for truth is known as 'Socratic irony'. At the heart of the method is an eager quest for truth through reason, which is the philosophical foundation of rationalism.

These thought processes gave me clues to exploring the questions about human nature that settled so heavily on my psyche all those years ago when Takeshi died. In the following pages I will correlate some of the main ideas I encountered when tracing the outlines of the evolution of Greek philosophy.

Knowledge of Ignorance

The Roman philosopher and politician Cicero, who lived some three hundred years after Socrates, talked about Socrates as the first to 'bring philosophy down from heaven to earth'. Given Cicero's own monumental and humane intellect, his recognition of Socrates only confirms the giant step the 'gadfly of Athens' made in the classical world. But Cicero's homage also tells us something else.

In ancient Greece prior to Socrates, problems of ethics, morals, truth and the essence of things were generally felt to be beyond mortal minds. Having established a pantheon and a set of traditions regarding the ways of the gods and their interactions with humans (the Greek myths), people effectively erased the big, ultimate questions from their consciousness, leaving them for the gods to decide. In dismissing the myths as fiction, the sophists may have been the first in distinguishing myth from truth, even before Socrates. But Socrates was the first rationalist after millennia of human history to bring ultimate questions to the fore, define them and demonstrate the human potential for rational thought about them.

More interesting, however, is to consider how Socrates himself embraced a rationalist approach in considering the unchanging reality of man and nature. Yes, his was a brilliant mind, but his application of reason to consideration of truth and essence did not take shape without substance. Why was he so certain that reason could illuminate truth?

In grappling with such basic questions as why people live and what constitutes immutable truth, Socrates shunned easy answers. Instead, he focused on knowledge: humans are equipped to consider those questions using reason, but they simply cannot grasp the truth of things without rational discipline. He called himself 'an ignorant being'. As for the sophists, he exposed their pretentious show of knowledge as ignorance cloaked in erudition. A person with true knowledge would never accept a sophist attitude. At the heart of the Socratic dicta, 'I know only that I know nothing' and 'Know thyself', lies the belief that knowledge begins with awareness of ignorance.

Precisely in recognizing his own ignorance, hence his ability to know little about the truth or essence of things without great effort, Socrates grasped the essential reality of his ignorance. This became the one truth now available to him. Though it seems a paradoxical way of viewing truth, Socrates used the exercise of reason to discern that one essential quality of being human was ignorance, thereby attaining knowledge of at least that fact. Thus did Socrates become convinced that truth could be known only through reason. It was his first step as a rationalist. It also marked a pivotal point of departure from the scepticism the sophists had implanted in many Athenian minds. Socrates determined that although ignorant, he acknowledged the fact of his ignorance and because of that he was at least wiser than the sophists, who, without knowing any truths at all, depended solely on persuasion through eloquence. The self-awareness that 'I know only that I know nothing' – the core of the so-called Socratic paradox – signifies no negation of reason or sense of resignation towards gaining knowledge; rather, it propels Socrates onto a path of positive enquiry into the true nature of things.

From the moment he knew that he knew nothing, Socrates went on to patiently spur and provoke his pupils into recognizing the fact of their own ignorance. He established a blueprint of reasoning and an inquisitorial procedure that strongly influenced philosophers up to the early modern era. Suffice it to note here that the Socratic approach generated fundamental questions that were taken up by subsequent generations of philosophers.

Let us now explore the idea, 'I know only that I know nothing'. The Socratic awareness of ignorance, I believe, opens a channel to understanding the core element, that essence of human nature I intuited in my adolescent encounter with death.

The Dualism of Ignorance

Using rational thought, Socrates deduced that to be human is to be ignorant and with that discovery he demonstrated the reality of ignorance. But if people are wholly ignorant they can never know the ultimate reality of their world – including the truth of their own ignorance. In that case, my moment of intuition in junior high school when I experienced intimations of philosophical truths could never have happened.

Suppose people had no sense at all of a uniquely, essentially human nature. Would not the ancient Greeks who confronted death have plunged into a final hedonistic rush to experience every available pleasure? In the face of imminent death, if a man decided to dedicate his remaining days on earth to study, would he not have been ridiculed for squandering time?

About a century before Socrates, in the city-state of Sparta, there lived a poet named Tyrtaios. His was poetry of nobility and beauty in death, typified by the fall of a young warrior defending his country and freedom. Tyrtaios gave words to the ancient ideal of the soldier who proudly gave his life in battle. He glorified the military spirit that demanded a brave man die a heroic death rather than cling to life or resent its end. The poems are filled with the vibrant force of the pure and single-minded mission to give one's life in defence of the homeland. That was honour, the hallmark of the true hero.

Interspersed in literature from the centuries prior to Socrates, ideas like those, vaunting selfless loyalty at times of war or other crises, resonated with echoes of some essential quality in human nature. Although the majority of the population was still acquiescent in the interpretation by the gods of philosophical questions about life and truth by the gods, there were also those who, in the face of imminent death, renounced worldly pleasures in favour of a noble cause. But in Tyrtaios's day, rationalist ideas explaining *why* a person would feel drawn towards self-transcending action had yet to appear. That philosophy would not take shape until the time of Socrates.

In any case it can be argued that if people in those days were not aware of an essential, purely human nature, the reason was not because it did not exist, but because its existence had not yet been discovered. While both are forms of 'not knowing', they have radically different meanings.

Consider an example from the history of science: the law of universal gravitation. Until its discovery by Isaac Newton through his studies of physical motion, gravity was unknown to science, but no Newtonian breakthrough was necessary to teach people that apples fell from their branches. Presumably even our most ancient ancestors knew perfectly well that you have to hold tight to the trunk when you climb a tree – otherwise you fall. Before Newton's exposition, the law of universal gravitation clearly existed in our physical surroundings. People experienced it, even if they could not define it.

The same can be said of essential human nature. Socrates argued that truth and the essence of things could be grasped through reason precisely because they existed. Essential human nature existed. It had always been profoundly present and active, but before Socrates people were blind to the possibility of knowing what it was. Socrates, like Newton, had merely uncovered the existence of an essential nature, not invented it.

One eventually reaches a point in tracing the course of Socrates' thinking where it seems that no further analysis is possible. There remains the stark question of the existence or non-existence of ultimate reality regardless of whether or not people are aware of it. To come down on either side is the philosophical equivalent of the axioms of geometry; they encapsulate a basic understanding not open to any further explanation.

In Euclidean geometry the theorem 'the sum of a triangle's interior angles is 180 degrees' can be proven using auxiliary lines, vertical angles, corresponding angles and so on. The proposition 'parallel lines never meet' however, is an axiom, a basic mathematical premise taken to be absolutely true even though its truth or fallacy may be practically impossible to prove. That axiom is an indispensable theoretical tool in solving problems in Euclidean plane geometry. In the same sense, when Socrates proffered the axiom that the rational human mind can be aware of its ignorance ('I know only that I know nothing'), he gave subsequent philosophers an indispensable tool to engage in even more challenging problems.

The idea of instinct as part of human nature is in some respects like an axiom in geometry. It may be that something like instinct, a quality that people are born with, made Socrates employ reason as a way to pursue, as far as possible, truth and the essence of things. Later, when he was sentenced to die and had to decide how to respond, the position Socrates chose can also be explained by this belief in an axiom-like core of human nature. But before commenting on Socrates' death let us briefly resist/ reconsider [recapitulate] the method he expounded to contemplate the essential in human nature.

The starting point is an awareness of one's ignorance, creating the germ of an intellectual need to at least think about the as-yet indiscernible essential nature of what it is to be human. Sustaining that need one perseveres, moving closer and closer to some understanding. Even though the essence of being human [humanness] does not immediately become clear the quest for truth is not abandoned to the gods, as when myths were still vested with authority. Nor does one concede all to doubt, as did the sceptics. Socrates assures us that precisely because we acknowledge our ignorance we can think deeply for ourselves about the true nature of being human [humanness].

Many, if not most people, have at some time asked themselves eternal questions like, 'Why do people exist?' Such questions arouse a philosophical urge present in all of us, like an instinct. Even if the truth that such questions seek is not immediately apparent, it is not because the truth does not exist, but because its existence is well concealed. 'Ignorance of unreality' and 'ignorance of reality' are clearly two very different concepts.

The Death of Socrates

In 399 BC an Athenian court condemned Socrates to death for denying the existence of the gods and corrupting youth, among other charges. According to contemporary accounts his students and friends implored him, in his jail cell, to petition for a pardon and the court gave him the option of a suspended sentence if he left Athens.

Plato confirms, however, that Socrates refused either to plead for a pardon or accept exile from Athens. He consciously elected to die. Why? First, to admit the charges against him and seek a pardon would have been to concede that the ideas he had given his best years to teaching the people of Athens were wrong. Second, if he had accepted permanent exile from Athens it would have invalidated his ideas and discredited his philosophy. So he stood firm in an unfaltering commitment to the pursuit of truth, that which is real even though we are ignorant of it. Socrates' principles were sufficiently strong and well-founded that he was prepared to sacrifice his life for them.

His disciples and students were disconsolate, imploring him in prison to take whatever action necessary to save himself so that he could continue teaching the way of reason. Socrates refused. He would not compromise and had determined to die. When his friends and students argued – rationally – that since he stood to lose everything by dying, it would be wiser in this case to concede a little, Socrates rejected the suggestion out of hand. Finally, submitting to the verdict of the Athenian jury, Socrates drank the hemlock.

Certainly I am not alone in seeing in this act a profound sense of mission in regard to truth. At the time of his death, Socrates' faith in his convictions was sure, founded on an obdurate force of will that no one could shake. His mission paramount, he maintained his beliefs even when it became a lonely struggle against impossible odds. The story is filled with pathos and noble motives, but one also has the sense that Socrates found a quiet satisfaction in behaviour that he knew carried a mortal risk. Perhaps his reward was an inner [conviction] that, to his contemporaries and to future generations, he was confirming through his death that truth exists and therefore could be discerned.

In my mind, the images of Socrates staking his life on his beliefs and Takeshi looking ahead to his death from terminal illness somehow overlapped. Socrates was prepared to die and thus affirm his convictions about truth. Takeshi threw himself into study even while knowing he would soon be gone from this world. These two responses struck me as connected, expressions of something shared over the almost two and a half millennia that separated them.

What was that element I felt in both Socrates and Takeshi? Perhaps I was hearing a cry from deep within the heart, the voice of some irresistible compulsion arising in the face of imminent death. I saw in both a powerful sense of purpose rooted in a highly self-aware and self-determined philosophy that let them dare to do, of their own free will, what would be extremely difficult had they simply been ordered to so do. Furthermore, in the actions of these two people confronting their own death there was no disjunction between the self and the philosophy embraced by the self. Perhaps truth as apprehended through reason shows its true form in the crisis of imminent death, and the test of its authenticity emerges as the dying person struggles to decide how to spend the life that remains. Ultimately it may be that the urge to contribute, which is what gives rise to that sense of purpose, is something that everyone, without exception, experiences when becoming aware that the end of their life is approaching.

Something else that struck me was the trace of satisfaction discernible in Socrates' determination not to flee or recant but to die. From where did that satisfaction arise? Perhaps he saw the acts of his final days as the perfecting of the philosophical practice through which he had tried to show the nature of truth as he understood it in his innermost being. It is as if he had taken upon himself a mission; in choosing such a death he hoped to demonstrate that the essence of human nature can be discovered through reason, and to prove to his contemporaries and to future generations that such immutable essences truly exist.

But whatever Socrates' intentions may have been, such a selfless sense of mission does not always override the instinctive pursuit of pleasure. Nor do I wish to judge the worth of a person by which of these dominates the spirit. Not everyone can emulate Socrates, nor can everyone be expected to face death like Takeshi. Throughout history many people, upon realizing their life was coming to an end, undoubtedly chose the path of hedonism to the moment of death. That choice, in fact, is probably the more common one.

However, the crucial point I am trying to make is that although some choose to serve the greater good or an altruistic cause while others abandon themselves to pleasure-seeking, both types experience the same undeniable upsurge of desire and vigorous sense of purpose to contribute something to the world. I am convinced that these feelings arise in everyone, without exception, when they become aware that death is near, which means that all people experience them at least once in their lives. Even those who choose to deal with imminent death in the pursuit of pleasant diversions do so, not because they do not care about contributing or have no purpose, but because even though they have such feelings they elect not to act upon them.

In summation, what led me gradually to appreciate the essential, shared human experience of what I term an 'urge to contribute' and 'sense of purpose' was my encounter with convictions that endured to the point of death. I found those convictions in the spiritual energy that compelled both Socrates and, some 2,400 years later, Takeshi, to face impending death in the singular manner each did.

Plato's Ideal Forms

Perhaps the single most important lesson for us in Socrates' death is a refutation of conventional wisdom; by his actions Socrates confounded the commonly accepted view that no one meets death gladly. Going one step further, his particular consciousness of his own death, and Takeshi's also, did not spring from a view of the world as transitory or meaningless, but from understanding based on reason. To apprehend death in the way Socrates did was, on the contrary, to be liberated from a sense of the evanescence of things.

Put another way, Socrates and Takeshi achieved by reason what most people cannot do and usually do not even attempt. Each acted in accord with his philosophical principles and for that reason was able to discover a self free from nihilistic despair. Through their deaths I learned of the profound satisfaction that comes with being truly in harmony with one's philosophy, and found my first real clues to the essential nature of human beings.

We have to bear in mind that the choices that Socrates and Takeshi made involved an essential element of human nature that, like the axioms of geometry, stands as given, self-evident, not subject to further explanation. When people act upon a sense of purpose, they are acting from an irresistible, unavoidable force that wells up in their hearts compelling them to choose a specific course of action. That force, a quality of human nature, is the urge to contribute.

As I continued to explore this line of thought I realized that this sense of purpose is an irreplaceable feeling that people experience when they recognize the innate urge to contribute. Also, in deconstructing the relationship between the urge to contribute and sense of purpose, I came to suspect that these notions pointed towards yet another new discovery.

All of this happened during my student days. I still did not fully understand but it seemed to me that among the various ways in which the urge to contribute is manifested, there are times when it is expressed as a sense of purpose compelling people to undertake challenges normally considered too daunting. To follow that kind of mission, I surmised, would have to generate a unique sense of fulfillment. Furthermore, the urge to contribute, far from emerging only in moments of individual crisis, might also operate during broader historical or environmental crises – whether in the past or anticipated in the future – to preserve the ties linking all forms of life.

As I saw it, something deep inside gives people the strength to confront seemingly insurmountable problems, a strength that presumably we, too, will bequeath to future generations. Over thousands of years of history humans have drawn on this powerful force in withstanding critical predicaments and I believe the source of this force is the innate urge to contribute, in all its various manifestations. Just as applying an auxiliary line to a problem of geometry can, in one stroke, yield the solution, recognizing the existence of the urge to contribute is like finding a key to understanding the true nature of human life.

In any case, before I could concentrate on the various elements that come into play during the crisis of imminent death bringing the urge to contribute to the surface, I had to think more constructively about my initial query; in the case of someone who does not have long to live, but is freed from feeling life's evanescence and has overcome the fear of death, how does that person spend the rest of his or her life? As I tried to clarify what implications these conjectures had in relation to the essence of humanity, I was able to ground my notion of the 'urge to contribute' in ideas that emerged from my study of philosophy. The ancient Chinese philosophers Mencius and Xunzi, among others, also explored the question of essential human nature. Mencius argued that it was fundamentally good while Xunzi saw it as inherently evil. For our present purposes, however, let us follow the line of ancient Greek philosophers – in particular Socrates' student Plato – to see what they have made of this conundrum of the essential nature of the human being.

Plato's philosophy is in some ways mystical, containing elements that today are sometimes difficult to accept. It nonetheless remains a powerful system of thought that must be considered in any attempt to elucidate the ultimate ends towards which our inner lives are oriented.

Socrates sought to use reason to gain the deepest possible understanding of ultimate reality, that which is always absolutely true no matter when, where, or by whom it is grasped. Plato, his student and contemporary, took this approach several steps further.

Plato taught that flesh-and-blood human beings and the essential or ideal form of human being existed in different realms. That separation between the real/phenomenal and the essential/ideal applied to all things. A particular dog, cat, or an instance of the beautiful, for example, existed in one realm, while in their ideal forms Dog, Cat, and Beauty existed in another. He thus posited the existence of two realms, the mundane realm of the things around us and another realm of essences, or Ideal Forms of all the phenomena we perceive in the mundane world.

In philosophy this view is known as dualism. Over and against the natural world of perceptible reality Plato constructs an invisible, ideal world – the realm of Ideas, or perfect Forms – and everything in the natural world is a particular instance of and is modelled on an Ideal Form. Using examples, he argues that while we can directly perceive the phenomenal, visible world, the realm of Forms is beyond our direct perception, our only access to it is through reason. To that extent Plato agrees with Socrates that reason provides access to truth and ultimate reality. But whereas Socrates indicated the path to ultimate reality without describing that realm, Plato offered a more comprehensive and clearer picture, presenting it as the realm of Ideal Forms.

Plato's epistemological argument is in a way a radical departure from the attitude towards knowledge of thinkers in previous generations, who tended to sweep questions of ultimate reality or truth under the carpet of myth. His thinking also diverges acutely from that of the sophists, who argued a kind of situation-contingent morality; what was right or wrong, just or unjust, and so on, was not incontrovertible but in constant flux, varying from one place or time to the next.

In Plato's system, the objects and phenomena of the visible world – people, animals, beauty, morality, and so on – undergo constant change, arising and disappearing, but the realm of Forms is eternal and unchanging. Plato is careful in observing the phenomenal world, the world of perceptions, but is more interested in, and values more highly, the invisible realm of Forms as the source of the eternal laws underlying all natural phenomena and human activity wherever and whenever they occur.

The Path to Certain Knowledge – Episteme

Although we can experience through our senses the everyday world around us – the world of perception – simply by opening our eyes and ears, the world of Forms can be accessed only through reason. Without reason it is almost impossible to imagine, much less to 'see'. Contained in Plato's Republic is an allegory known as the Myth of the Cave, created to provide a metaphorical way to understand the difference between the two realms. In this allegory, Plato proposes that just as things in the mundane world around us cast shadows, so specific instances of Ideal Forms are projected as the things of this phenomenal world. I would like to offer a slightly modified version of the cave allegory that might help to clarify Plato's concept of the realm of Forms.

In ancient times a certain tribe of people lived in a large cave. Every day as the sun began to set in the west, a watchman would build a fire at the cave's entrance. This was done partly to ward off the darkness and partly for another reason – to project shadows onto the back wall of the cave. The cave people were concerned that wild animals or enemy tribesmen might creep into the cave at night, or that their own children might wander out, and so they kept their eyes on the back wall in case a shadow was cast by anything or anyone moving around the entrance. If a wolf or tiger tried to enter the cave its shadow would alert the people inside, who would move quickly to minimize potential damage by the animal. Similarly, if any person passed in front of the fire – a child straying into the dangerous woods outside, or enemy tribesmen trying to peek inside the cave – their shadows, too, would loom up as enlarged images on the cave's back wall and the inhabitants could spring quickly into action. From time to time the cave-dwellers held training sessions; they passed hand-made figures in front of the fire so that the people could practice identifying them from the shadows they cast. During one such session what seemed to be the shadow of an animal loomed up on the wall, the image fluttering as the flames of the fire flickered. The tribesman whose turn it was to identify the source of the image answered that it was a wolf, while the next one said it must be a tiger. The figure was then slowly turned until its full profile was clearly out-lined in the shadow on the back wall. Obviously the person who had answered 'tiger' was wrong because the shadow showed the unmistakable pointed snout of a wolf, not the large head of a tiger.

Inside the cave, there was also a sequestered area which served as a prison where youths of a rival tribe lived as captives. Having been captured in infancy and kept in this prison since then these youths had, in effect, never seen the world outside the cave. The silhouettes cast onto the cave wall were their only form of infor-mation about the outside world. From years of watching the shadow-recognition training sessions they acquired detailed knowledge of the kinds of shadows cast by wolves, tigers and various other beings from the outside world but had never seen an actual wolf or tiger.

Early one morning, one of the prisoners, at the risk of his life, resolved to attempt an escape from the cave. During a momen-tary lapse in the guard's vigilance he slipped past the entrance fire – the source of light for the images that had been his only access to the outside world – and stole out of the cave. He ran straight across a vast expanse of land, the details of which gradually emerged from the gloom in the rising glow of dawn. Fording a stream and passing through a forest he saw the real world with his own eyes for the first time. Real wolves, real tigers – everything in the dazzling scene appeared to his eyes a thing of inexpressible beauty. To see in their actual forms the real objects and animals he had until then known only as shadows gave him immeasurable joy.

Before long, however, the fleeing youth was overtaken by his pursuers, struck down by an arrow and dragged, gasping, back to the cave prison. There, in a strained, feeble voice, his dying words to his fellow prisoners were, 'I had to see the reality behind the shadows'.

In Platonic terms, what this man risked his life for was *episteme*, the Greek concept of certain, demonstrable knowledge (as opposed to opinion). Plato thus hypothesizes in the *Republic* that everything we perceive in this mundane world is but a 'shadow' of ultimate reality, just as the prisoners living in the cave see only shadow-images of actual beings. Moreover, people who have known only shadows feel a profound yearning for the real world from which those images are cast. Plato's realm of Ideal Forms can thus be understood as being, for us, what the vast, dazzling land outside the cave was to the escaped prisoner, who, despite knowing nothing but the shadows of that reality, nonetheless longed for and finally experienced.

Forms as Templates

The gap between ultimate reality and what we normally perceive as reality can also be illustrated in terms of dimension. Imagine people who exist in a two-dimensional world; to such people most of the realities of the three-dimensional world we inhabit would be incomprehensible. If someone in that flat realm were to start walking in a straight line from a certain spot, he or she could never return to that starting point without changing course. We in the three-dimensional world however, know that if we continue on a straight course along the same longitude, moving perpendicular to the Earth's axis and onwards, we will eventually return to the spot from where we started. Perhaps it is because of a similar difference of 'dimension' that we who live in the world of perceptible reality find it difficult to comprehend the realities of the realm of Forms.

In Plato's view, Forms are the models or moulds from which the things of the mundane world are made. Another explanation is that the things of the world are not themselves true beings but only the shadows or silhouettes cast by true beings, that is by Ideal Forms. Specific, mortal wolves, tigers and people of our world change and fade away with the passage of time and though we perceive them with our senses, such sensory perception does not provide access to their true reality. At our mundane level of reality, individual wolves, for example, are born and eventually die; they are imperfect beings, or shadows of an Ideal Form that sooner or later pass out of existence.

Through the voice of a character in *Macbeth*, William Shakespeare describes human existence in this world:

> Life's but a walking shadow, a poor player that struts and frets his hour upon the stage, and then is heard no more; it is a tale told by an idiot, full of sound and fury, signifying nothing. (*Macbeth*, V.v)

In the Platonic view, although our everyday world is just such an illusory 'tale told by an idiot', all the animals and things in it are created in imitation of the eternal forms (essences) in the timeless realm of Forms. Furthermore, traces of these essences are faintly apparent, even from the mundane world, to those who apply their minds to apprehending the truth.

Plato also surmises that, should we apprehend the true Form (essence) of Wolf, for example, it is not because we empirically recognize it from our experience of imperfect, individual wolves but rather because we have an abiding memory, somewhere in our reason, of this Form as the original template of all wolves. The place where all such templates exist is what Plato calls the realm of Forms. This realm contains the templates or ideal types in imitation of which all particular instances (specific objects and phenomena of the world of perception) come into being. The templates Human Being, Animal, Beauty and so on in the realm of Forms give rise to individual human beings, animals and instances of natural beauty in the world of perception. The latter are not eternal beings but only transient particular instances, or tokens. The templates in the realm of Forms, however, are both perfect and eternal. They are the permanent and immutable essences or ultimate reality, which Plato believed we can access through reason.

In the world of perception individual wolves, moulded from the Wolf template gradually move further and further away from the Ideal Form. No matter how many of these imperfect wolves we observe we cannot by such empirical observation alone arrive at an understanding of the complete, true essence of ideal, eternal 'wolf-ness'. But even while inhabiting the world of perception, somewhere in our rational minds we have an etched memory of the Wolf-Form which we knew in our previous existence in the realm of Forms and which we sometimes strive to recollect. We make this effort to recollect because we are intermittently compelled by an instinct to know the truth behind appearances, just like the cave prisoner who escaped to find the actual things he had formerly known only by their shadows.

The ancient Greeks strove to capture the beauty of the human body in sculpture. Though inhabiting this imperfect world of perception, they tried to attain and express perfect beauty that remains unchanged in all times and places. In other words, the sculptors of ancient Greece aspired to true knowledge of the ideal Beauty in the realm of Forms.

Consider, for example, the Venus de Milo, named after the Greek island of Melos (Milo), where it was excavated. The face of this Venus has many of the features – the high brow, the line of the nose extending almost straight down from the brow, and so on – prevalent in both male and female statues sculpted around the same time. Also typical of Hellenistic depictions of the human body, the head is rendered slightly smaller than normal and the body as a whole is twisted into a slight vertical spiral. These devices capture a sense of beauty common to both sexes; from this we may presume that the sublime beauty of this ideal form, though never fully embodied in any actual person, remains constant in our aesthetic sensibility.

For us living in this world of perception, reason – our capacity to think rationally – is essential to any effort to approximate an understanding of the ultimate reality of things. In Plato's view, at the moment our souls 'descend' at birth into the world of perception, we forget all of the things we knew in our prior existence in the world of Forms and thus we become estranged from episteme, or certain knowledge. This idea at first seems to be a regression to the kind of mythical thinking prevalent before Plato but the crucial difference is that Plato, as a rationalist, believed that by the exercise of reason and only by reason, can people 'recollect' the world of Forms forgotten at birth.

Plato established the world's first university in the grove of Academos in Athens. From its location the university later came to be known as the Academeia or the Academy. The entrance to the Academy bore the inscription *Ageometretos medeis eisito*: 'Let no one unversed in geometry enter here'. Plato believed that episteme – true and certain knowledge – could in part be attained through the study of mathematics (geometry) because the objects of that study never change. That the sum of the internal angles of a triangle is 180 degrees, for example, is a fact that never changes or perishes. Likewise, it is an eternal and constant truth that the angle formed by drawing lines from the two points where a diagonal intersects the circumference of a circle to another point on the circumference will always be a right angle. All such mathematical axioms are immutable and true regardless of when, where, or by whom they are studied.

When we human beings arrive at the sole correct solution to a problem in geometry, it is not because of our empirical experience but because rational thought enables us to find the solution. With our minds we use reason to gain access to truth. It is as though, in accord with the Platonic notion, people have a prior existence in a world of Forms, forget the truths of that world the moment they are born into this one and then recollect them through reason. This rationalist view contrasts with the philosophy of empiricism, which, in its strictest sense, holds that people can acquire an understanding of the truth solely through experience, that all knowledge is *a posteriori*.

Inheriting Socrates' conviction that through reason we can achieve a grasp of ultimate reality, Plato sought to elucidate aspects of truth and ultimate reality in terms of his theory of Forms. Far from only abstract theorizing, his philosophy contains important clues on how people should live their lives. Let us explore Plato's line of thought a little further.

The Yearning of Eros

The key points of Plato's philosophy covered so far can be summarized as follows:

Existence is divided into two realms or planes: the world of perception, which we see and feel around us, and the realm of Ideal Forms, which contains the essences or true, perfect forms of the particular things apparent to us in the world of perception.

Plato considers in detail how these two worlds interact:

Humans in some way exist simultaneously in both worlds. The two worlds do not coexist within each person, but rather are ordered and linked through reason. Existing without essence amid other transient phenomena, people have only one tool with which to gain access to the ultimate reality of Forms, namely, their faculty of reason.

From that basis, Plato explored when and how reason is activated in human understanding:

Each person's eternal soul once inhabited the realm of Forms.

Many people, however, have totally rejected Plato's theory of Forms. Aristotle, Plato's pupil, was highly critical of his teacher's doctrine of eternal Forms. On the other hand, Plato's quasimystic views on the soul, Forms and so on, were taken up by mystic thinkers from the medieval period to the Renaissance and absorbed into unique philosophical and aesthetic systems.

Upon being born into the world of perception, the soul forgets the truths with which it was previously well acquainted in the realm of Forms, but at times it becomes able to recollect them through its encounters with phenomena in the world of perception. Because of those fleeting recollections, the soul develops a profound yearning to return to its proper abode, namely, the realm of Forms.

Let us consider this last point about yearning to return to the world of ultimate reality. Plato describes it as the soul awaking from a sleep and, drawn by the intense attraction of Forms, strives to return to the ideal world. Plato calls this attraction eros. In my version of the cave allegory it is this attraction, this yearning, that compels the young prisoner to risk death to escape from the cave and see the realities behind the shadows. His escape can be interpreted as the response to an irresistible eros-yearning impulse for truth that outweighed all other considerations and motivations.

At the same time we must bear in mind that the picture Plato paints of such a committed truth-seeker is an ideal one. In reality, few people are willing to risk their lives to discover 'truth' or 'ultimate reality' and many consider the very act of risking one's life to be wrong.

The point here, however, is that human beings, whether they are exceptional people filled with an eros-type yearning for truth or ordinary people who are largely oblivious to the way of reason, experience moments of being held in thrall by the allure of absolute truth or ultimate reality. Even without recourse to the theory of Forms, we know from experience that such moments occur in people's lives – as in, for example, the inspiration experienced by artists. Plato paid special attention to such instances and sought to explain their meaning in terms of eternal Forms.

The Platonic Tripartite Soul

At a purely affective level, to me Plato's ideas are more redolent of art than of philosophy. Naturally I recognize the immense impact of Plato's thought on the subsequent history of philosophy. Nonetheless, I find the venerable figures of Greek philosophers in certain art works all the more beautiful for their evocation of the 'upper world' that Plato described. A good example is the 'School of Athens', a fresco painted by the Renaissance master Raphael in the Stanza della Segnatura (Room of the Segnatura) in the Pontifical Palace of the Vatican. Whether we contemplate Plato's realm of Forms or the *hyperouranos* (hyper-heaven) where the realm of Forms was believed to exist, Plato clearly envisaged such a realm to be one of absolute, perfect beauty, or rather the ultimate Ideal Form of Beauty itself.

Plato also described eros as a form of mania, denoting eros as a human instinct, latent and powerful. In many of his writings Plato shows a keen interest in eros as an impulse towards the appreciation of beauty.

The yearning for truth also resembles what I described earlier (in the section headed 'The Death of Socrates') as an urge to contribute and sense of purpose that surface in circumstances of extreme crisis, such as the realization of impending death. Like other human instincts, these two feelings appear to exist in potential form in all people – truth-seekers and pleasure-seekers alike – and to well up spontaneously in life-and-death situations. In many

Philosophers of ancient Greece
– based on Raphael's *School of Athens*. What does the modern world
make of the figure of Plato pointing up toward the heavens?

such cases, that sense of purpose rises in people to lift them out of nihilism and despair over life's meaninglessness. Similarly, the urge to contribute often remains active in our consciousness in such dire crises, and acting upon that instinct can save us from the fear of death.

Directing the human intellect towards Forms can be regarded as ultimately the effect of eros, an instinctive striving for the beautiful. In the Platonic view, all ultimate realities, which only reason can apprehend, whether the structures of geometry or the ideal Wolf-Form, are constructs of perfect, harmonious beauty, like the 'mathematics of the gods'. Intuitively sensing ultimate truth and beauty even from within the perceptual world, the Platonic soul, quickened by the instinct of eros, aspires to the world of Forms.

Plato also argued that underlying all Forms is a special, ultimate Form, which he called the Good. All other Forms aspire to and are directed towards the Form of the Good. Not only those things of the ideal realm but also human beings in the perceptual world are propelled by an eros-type impulse towards ultimate beauty, to ascend a spiritual spiral staircase leading to the ultimate goal of full apprehension of the essence of ideal beauty, the Good. Put simply, human beings are by nature designed to yearn for and love the Good.

Now let us consider my own philosophical speculations in terms of Plato's theory. I posit that a psychological instinct, which I call the urge to contribute, operates in people even in the face of impending death, releasing them from the fear of death and thereby engendering a sense of purpose that enables them to undertake challenges they would otherwise avoid. This idea seems to be in conjunction with Plato's theory that people have an inbred tendency to love the Good.

Plato also maintains that the human soul is a composite of three often discordant parts: reason (*logos*), the soul's means of gaining access to the Good; spirit (*thumos*), the soul's force of will;

and desire (*epithumia*), the seat of the soul's appetites. For people living in the world of perception, the source of troubles concerning the ultimate reality we cannot see is in the disharmony between these three aspects of the soul. Specifically, the problem is the impeding of reason, either by an excess of spirit, whereby reason can no longer control spirit, or by an excess of desire, leading to indolence. In the soul's ideal state, each of its three parts is naturally oriented towards the Good, but in the bodily person they are frequently so out of balance that reason loses control of the other two and we stray from the path leading to the Good.

In the dialogue *Phaedrus*, Plato argues that reason must maintain control over spirit and desire. His concept of the ideal relationship between the three can be thought of as a chariot, with spirit and desire as the horses pulling it and reason as the driver. As long as the charioteer maintains control, rampant spirit is transformed into courage and intemperate desire into moderation. Only when reason is in control can the chariot stay on course towards the ultimate goal of the Good.

What I call sense of purpose corresponds to the spirit-horse, which in turn can be likened to an upsurge of eros. In Platonic terms, the sense of purpose that I intuitively recognized in the way Takeshi spent his final days can be understood as the instinct of spirit striving towards the world of Forms and sublimated to courage by the reins of reason. For Takeshi, reason was in control, steering his chariot towards the Good. In that moment the young man's instinctive urge to contribute found full expression in a sublime sense of purpose, a consciousness of mission.

What about someone who knows death is near and chooses the hedonistic way for the remainder of his or her life? In that circumstance, the desire-horse is out of control and dominant, causing the soul's chariot to swerve down the path of intemperance. To the pleasure-seeker, the reality of the urge to contribute exists but is unknown, something that remains difficult to grasp and hidden from view. But even in this situation within the soul the component of reason still tries to contain unruly spirit and capricious desire. If the charioteer 'reason' is too weak to control its mounts, this is the failure of a rational faculty that nonetheless *does exist* and thus is not attributable to its non-existence.

The Urge to Contribute and Enquiry into Human Nature

The rationalist approach taught by Socrates blossomed into full maturity in the philosophy of Plato. But however great the legacy Plato has bequeathed to Western philosophy I cannot help feeling something strained and artificial in my attempt to correlate his theory of Forms with my intuitions about the true nature of human being.

In fact, it was not through Plato's bequest that I came to view the urge to contribute as an instinct. Rather, I arrived at this understanding – that this feeling is a natural instinct that tends to be manifested in crises such as impending death – through a complex process of reflection and speculation. And it was on the basis of certain personal convictions that I postulated, as lying behind the sense of purpose gained through reason, an instinctive urge to contribute, the essential quality of human beings that qualifies them as *Homo contribuens*. Indeed, at various pivotal junctures in my life I have sensed that an instinctive urge to contribute ultimately gives rise to a sense of purpose, or a sense of mission.

Although these ideas were not derived directly from the philosophy of Plato, I suspect that this aspect of human instinct, which I discovered through Takeshi's death, is closely related to what in rationalist philosophy distils to the essence of human being. In examining the concept of the urge to contribute as instinct with reference to the philosophy of these great founders of Western rationalism, I was perhaps seeking confirmation of my own philosophical intuitions.

Hyperouranos
– based on the ruins of the Acropolis of Athens. *Hyperouranos*, the realm of Ideal Forms. How wonderful it would be to be able to soar up to that realm toward the Form of the Good.

Unlike other animals, at least in the widest sense, humans are social beings who live in a state of dependence on cultural and other systems of our own creation. Coincidentally we are, like other animals, nurtured by the natural world. Invariably, however, we are disorderly beings, out of kilter, not only within ourselves but also in relation to the natural environment. Therefore, in light of the spiritual and environmental degeneration of the present time, the ideas elaborated by Socrates and Plato deserve renewed attention. But we must go even further: without disparaging the great achievement that such ancient philosophy represents in the study of human nature, people today must aspire to establishing a new philosophical framework for our times by our own rational efforts.

Focusing on these key thinkers at the dawn of Western philosophy and on their exposition of the crucial importance of reason, this record of my inquiry into the essential nature of human beings is dedicated to helping to construct such a new philosophy. That essential nature – which I first intuitively glimpsed as a boy and have been contemplating virtually every day since – can be summarized in terms of sense of purpose and the instinctive urge to contribute, in the following way.

Human beings by nature cherish their instincts. At the moment when, through a direct instinctive sense, we are released from feelings of life's emptiness and futility, our instinctive urge to contribute transforms from a latent into an apparent reality. This urge to contribute often triggers, with a compelling instinct-like force, a sudden awakening of dormant reason; in some cases, like that of Takeshi, it activates a sense of purpose in a crisis situation. Particularly in the crisis of imminent death, this instinct liberates people from their fear of death. It can inspire with a strong sense of purpose that allows people to take on challenges normally too daunting. In society as a whole it can even generate a force potent enough to shape the character of the age.

Episode 1
Restaurant on the Point

Located about two hours' drive from central Tokyo, the restaurant was built right on the edge of a sheer coastal cliff. Affording a view of the entire bay, it was perched so high that first-time visitors recoiled as they glanced down from its panoramic windows at the ocean below. The waiter seated me at a window table. I had about half an hour until my daughter was due to arrive.

Even as I studied the menu the thought of the chasm beneath the jet-black, straight-grain floor made me reluctant to lower my feet. It was particularly unsettling because the sea was turbulent that day with the noise of wind and crashing waves roaring up through the vast space under the floor, up from the heaving deep-blue ocean far below.

By the time coffee arrived my uneasiness had passed. Gazing at the broad ocean and sipping my coffee I fell into a curious reminiscence on days long gone. I recalled the tobacco farms where I had lived for a few years as a child during the Second World War, in Kagawa on the island of Shikoku. Like many other children, I had been evacuated from Tokyo for my safety. To my urban eyes the farms had seemed immeasurably vast.

After the war I was brought back to Tokyo where I completed my education right through to university without once returning to Kagawa. Then, when I was twenty-two and about to graduate from university, I grew desperately homesick for those tobacco fields and returned to Kagawa for the first time since my childhood. The sun was setting as I reached the village I once knew as home and the sight of the eulalia spikes that covered the hills and fields, stained red in the sun's final glow, was like a waking vision. A short walk brought me to Shakuoji, the Buddhist temple where I used to play. I remembered leaping from one to the other of its round stepping-stones. Everything there, from the stone *komainu* (guard beasts) to the earth-plastered walls, was exactly as it had been when I was a boy.

But I realized then that something in me had changed, though I could not say why or under what influence that change had occurred. With this puzzling thought still not fully absorbed I set off for the tobacco farms. Before long they appeared dimly through the haze of eulalia flowers. I was struck by how that pastoral scene, which had seemed so vast when I was a child, had become miniaturized in my adult perception. I stood and gazed, marvelling at how much the simple elevation of my line of sight had transformed my impression of the entire scene.

Emerging from this reverie I turned from gazing out to sea and saw that inside the restaurant, on the stage at the back, a jazz band was just finishing its sound check. The black guitarist began playing an offbeat introduction; I had heard the same kind of music in New York the previous year. After a strong opening from the percussion and in time with the phrasing of the snare drum, the female vocalist eased into a gentle swing.

Sipping my still-warm coffee I pondered: Who has the right to arbitrarily decide that a certain height is either high or low? Even if that height were determined by some agreed standard to be 'high' , who has the right to judge it 'sublime'? Presumably the same goes for our concepts of happiness and unhappiness, wealth and poverty.

CHAPTER 2

HOMO CONTRIBUENS: ACTING OUT THE URGE TO CONTRIBUTE

ભ

We often do things for others in a spirit of selfless giving,
but whether or not we really understand the
feelings of the people we serve is another matter.

Like Trickling Water

Usually, people subconsciously adapt their behaviour with their own needs and interests foremost. We behave in this way to satisfy urges and desires that are essential to our lives. Certainly, enquiry into the reasons for our actions reveals the existence of instincts common to all people and with careful thought we realize that our own self-centred behaviour is bound to clash at times with that of others and at some point will become a cause for concern.

We know, however, that self-indulgent behaviour, insofar as it springs from natural instincts, is integral to our very existence and life. We also see that these instincts evident in ourselves are also apparent in everyone else.

Under the influence of these instinctive feelings human beings are more prone to be driven by hedonistic principles than ethical or moral standards. This tendency is not to be condemned or

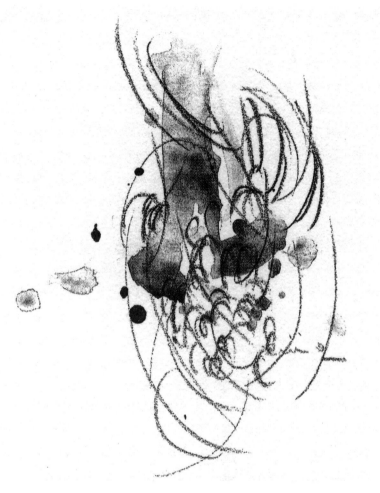

Falling water
– based on a drawing by Leonardo da Vinci in *Reonarudo da Vinchi sobyoshu* [Drawings by Leonardo da Vinci] (published by Iwanami Shoten, 1985). When simplified by rational intellect, even an apparently complex flow of water turns out to be no more than the collective motion of falling drops of water.

approved but regarded as a natural condition, just as ground water seeping through hidden cracks in thick bedrock naturally trickles down from higher to lower ground.

Even so, people tend to feel negative or even guilty about their own instincts. We are burdened with an inner conflict between the force of instincts arising from the individual self and the need to rationally control and deny those instincts in order to get by in the world and for guidance in this struggle we look to our immediate ethical and moral milieu. But control and denial are difficult to maintain. Even in thick bedrock, groundwater never gets trapped forever, nor does it ever flow upwards from lower to higher ground, since that would not be in accord with nature.

Humans are also social beings in a society whose context is coexistence and in which we restrain our individual instincts and admonish ourselves and each other against behaviour that puts individual desires first. This system of mutual admonition operates with the same firm force whatever the setting, whether among family, friends, or colleagues. We know that desires emanating from egocentric instinct can at times disrupt the equilibrium of social life.

In relation to any kind of social other, even a member of one's own family, one is always a self-centred self confronting a self-centred other and it is very rare for the two to achieve perfect harmony. Even when both suppress their individual instincts, there usually remains some degree of discord between the self and the other and when both put their own instincts, first outright conflict between them is inevitable.

Yet people learn how to suppress their instincts and can exercise this control when a situation demands. In one respect, one may well wonder why we do this. Total suppression of instinct is as unnatural as water trickling upwards. Instinct is not a dangerous weapon by which I might harm myself, in a sense it is myself.

Faced with this dilemma of our instincts, we may experience an awkwardness in our relationships with others, constantly doubting ourselves and embarrassed by our own impulses to seek pleasure. This is due to a natural resistance causing us to fail to recognize our instincts as natural functions.

Let us look more closely at the inner struggle of the self in this disoriented state. Though we are drawn in opposite directions by these inner forces of action and counteraction in the social context we may at some point begin to act in the interests of others. By contributing to the lives of others, whether family members or work colleagues, superiors or subordinates, we awaken to a kind of redeeming sense of rightness, and from that we derive peace of mind. This is because in such situations there is no denial of instinct, nor could acting in others' interests possibly be considered wrong.

In fact, this state of mind, stemming from our encounters with others, comes into effect spontaneously, like the operation of instinct, and does not violate any moral principle. With this the natural order of things is restored – the water is once again flowing as gravity dictates from high ground to low – and, without realizing, we find ourselves suffused with a natural sense of well-being. It is this innate human impetus to serve others that I call the urge to contribute.

The Urge to Contribute Is an Instinct

Instincts are innate capacities vested in us by nature to facilitate our lives. They are not something we intentionally acquire by learning. They are present in us, not because of human deliberation, but by the working of natural laws in human beings.

I regard the urge to contribute as an instinct and characterize it as arising from the psyche to differentiate it from mainly physiological instincts, such as hunger and sexual appetite. So, even though the concept of instinct is usually associated with physiology, I want to distinguish the two, physiological instincts and psychological instincts and identify the urge to contribute as among the latter. But both types of instinct exist naturally, in accordance with the laws that govern human life.

When acting altruistically, most of us make certain assumptions about the situation and the recipient. After doing something for someone, I tend, half-subconsciously, to presume that he or she will thank me, or at least feel grateful. I have tried to examine my feelings whenever I embark on an altruistic act and am quite certain that the sense of well-being experienced from wanting to help, or from helping, is not a learned response or a contrived consciousness. It is a state of mind wherein the sense of fulfilment seems to be instinctive. Conventional explanations concerning the motives for altruism seem artificial by comparison.

Since people tend so often to view instincts warily, as somehow base, we advise caution against complete surrender to such urges. We also realize, however, that in many respects our instincts are necessary for survival. Moreover, even the urge to contribute, to serve the interests of others, clearly embraces, like other instincts, a desire to satisfy oneself. Taking this to be the natural state of things I propose that the urge to contribute is an instinct peculiar to human beings. This is my basic position in regarding the urge to contribute as an instinct: altruistic behaviour, which at one level serves others' interests, also serves my own interests.

This opens up a whole new perspective, a previously imperceptible realm of mind that materializes with the realization that one literally lives by instinct. When I recognize the same urge to contribute in others and furthermore consider myself in relation to that instinct operating in others, I am filled with the poignant awareness that I am in many ways 'being enabled to live' .

This realization, which is neither optimistic nor negative, transcends all forms of discord and contradiction between the self and others, leaving one with a pure sense of well-being. This is not to argue that discord and conflict are thus completely eradicated, but beyond such real-world problems the realization that the self both lives and is 'enabled to live' engenders an unadulterated sense of fulfilment.

The Fifth 'Life Mode'

A person who is excessively self-centred is unable to understand another's suffering. That does not necessarily mean that the person who does try to help understands, either, but one thing we can say about the relationship between the self and others is that to give up on life and completely negate one's own existence, for whatever reason, does nothing for anyone, oneself or others. Despair only increases one's own isolation and that has a detrimental effect on the urge to contribute.

It is almost impossible to persuade someone who has given up on life to consider the needs and wants of others. This is because despair itself precludes the possibility of being ready to listen and any power of self-motivation diminishes. The person finds no real points of contact with others and is therefore impervious to persuasion.

Conversely, someone who strives to see things from another person's point of view, even if he or she encounters that person only once, can never succumb to despair. Such people draw on their inner instincts and the 'radar' of that heightened sensibility tells them, through that encounter, who and what the other is – someone with a personality different from their own, a different history, a different range of skills. They can even get an idea of the knowledge the other has acquired. To someone with this ability to discern the depth of another's being, even from a chance meeting, each and every other person becomes an entire cosmos.

An individual life can be thought of as the aggregate of a range of different modes or phases, like the oscillation phases that make up the spectra of light and sound. In my view this totality can be divided into the four general 'life modes' of play, learning, work, and daily life. Ultimately these four combine to characterize the individual's life as a whole but at the same time each can be separately distinguished from the others as a discrete mode unto itself. The modes have certain aspects in common but in other respects they conflict.

Each mode can be subdivided further. Play, for instance, embraces entertainment, sport, hobbies and travel. Learning incorporates formal study and practical experience, as well as the knowledge that comes from meeting people or reading books. Work may be an economic activity for one's livelihood or it might include, for example, some kind of local community service. Daily life encompasses a broad range of activities concerned with food, clothing and shelter.

From another perspective, each of the modes can be thought of as in some way inclusive, encapsulating some or all of the others. We could say, for example, that for some people the pursuit of play, learning and work are all oriented towards the overriding mode of daily life. To other people work may be the target mode to which the others are directed. Such people would say that they play, learn and attend to their daily needs all for the supreme cause of work. Similarly, either play or learning could be regarded as the primary or dominant mode supported by the others. It is thus difficult to ascribe distinct roles to the four life modes; each can be either an end or a means.

Thus each person can be expected to have a unique configuration of life modes. But that being so, what distinguishes the human species as a whole? The Dutch historian Johan Huizinga (1872–1945) focused on the mode of play as the defining essence of humans, which he accordingly termed *Homo ludens*, or 'man the player'. In biology, however, human beings are referred to as *Homo sapiens*, 'man the reasoner', for our peculiar capacity for advanced thinking and learning. And by emphasizing our ability to work (produce things), we can also characterize our species as *Homo faber*, 'man the maker'.

Yet another image of humanity emerges when we focus on the urge to contribute, which I identify as an instinct peculiar to and distinctive of human beings. This is the perspective that leads me to characterize humanity as *Homo contribuens*, (man the contributor) by which I mean humanity as an inclusive fellowship of mutual service. The term *Homo contribuens* thus evokes an aspect of being human that the other four modes – play, learning, work, and daily life – do not explain. Finally, the term incorporates the sense of the self both living and 'being enabled to live'.

The addition of this fifth life mode, the mode of contribution, affords a much brighter view of human life. It evokes the bonds that link people to each other, lends breadth to our lives and gives us a more vivid sense of who we are.

More succinctly, the first four life modes account only for the characteristic features of individual human life. When I consider the reality of my own life only in terms of those four modes, I cannot help feeling that something is missing in my sense of being. This is because the four-mode model constructs the life of the individual without taking into consideration the individual's social interaction. That model might appear to be objective, quantifiable, but it fails to convey the full spectrum of life modes that make up human life, or the full continuum of life's permutations and progress.

By adding to those four modes the fifth mode of contribution we have the capacity to formulate the overall shape of human life, including its unpredictability. As long as this fifth mode is kept active in some corner of the psyche it serves to increase our sense of fulfilment and satisfaction and, like an auxiliary line in geometry, helps us to identify which path to take in pivotal moments of hesitation or confusion.

The contribution mode also encompasses areas of human life that are not fully covered by the other four modes. An example is volunteer work, which does not fit comfortably into either the work or daily-life categories and cannot be properly deemed either play or learning. Then there are activities such as local community work, which is related to the work mode but is not economic activity in the accepted sense; spontaneous deeds for the benefit of others; acts performed in the context of parent-child relationships – and indeed all kinds of interpersonal relationships. The essential nature of these aspects of behaviour becomes clear when they are viewed in terms of the concept of *Homo contribuens*. I hope that by applying this concept to real-life cases and situations people will come to recognize and learn from this urge to contribute as it operates both in themselves and in others.

Choosing Life Modes

We often adapt our behaviour to the particular life mode we have chosen. A student, for example, transiting to the mode of learning, determines to concentrate his/her energies on that demanding role. Particularly when preparing for exams, the student's life mode is wholly oriented towards learning, as the distraction of play would be detrimental. However, to spend one's entire student life following nothing but scholarly pursuits would be exceedingly dull. The selection of a life mode reflects that person's needs, interests, and overall approach – it does not prescribe every detail. How, then, are these life modes determined, not simply for a specific period, such as one's student days, but for the entire span of a lifetime? How should we regard them and deal with them?

Just as we choose our clothes according to our individual tastes and needs so we are able to 'wear' this or that life mode as each occasion or period in life demands. An entire life is inevitably a composite of multiple life modes. The particular way this assimilation of multiple life modes occurs gives each individual life its unique flavour and vitality.

Certain modes are essential in the short term – assiduous devotion to study, for example, or a strict policy of never mixing work with pleasure. But an attempt to adopt any one mode for the whole of one's life would lead to stifling monotony and therefore defeat its own end. Adhering to a mode that should not be sustained too long is unlikely to bring true contentment.

People tend to enjoy what they do well. A level of expertise beyond the norm can be attained when work is enjoyable and learning or work can be approached with efficiency and enjoyment. That type of learning, therefore, is not rigid and formal, but ranges freely between the learning and play mode. The countless acts that make up an individual life can be seen as a composite spectrum of such multiple modes.

If you choose a life mode grounded in an instinctive motive – a deep-seated desire to do something – then within your overall spectrum that specific life mode will begin to transcend the others. On the other hand, if you become immersed in a single mode it will be difficult to sustain the behaviour that mode demands. This would be a life so bland and monochromatic as to be hardly worth calling a life.

Probing the Contribution Mode

As previously suggested, if we activate our instinctive urge to contribute in our life mode life would assume a much broader prospect. This proposition can be broken down into two parts: the premise, 'If we activate our instinctive urge to contribute in our life mode', and the conclusion, 'Our life takes on a much broader prospect'. To confirm one's own urge to contribute it is important to consider both the premise and the conclusion of this proposition in terms of one's own life.

First consider one's stance in relation to the urge to contribute. What I have called the five life modes are not merely tools to analyse your life as objective fact but are also guidelines indicating

The realm of intellectual life
– based on a drawing by Leonardo da Vinci in *Reonarudo da Vinchi sobyoshu* [Drawings by Leonardo da Vinci] (published by Iwanami Shoten, 1985). Human beings are unconsciously always thinking. But in order to make speculative judgements, we must have the axioms and tools of rational thought.

the avenues available at life's critical junctures. But how does one activate within oneself this intangible urge to contribute and gain a vivid sense of its working?

Generally, concepts are expressed through words but it is difficult to personalize them, to realize them as an active part of the self. How, then, can you realize within yourself the invisible urge to contribute? To analyse your 'self' and to understand its relation to others is crucial. Equally important are a sensitivity to phenomena that arise from unseen causes and an inquiring mind that seeks the essential nature inherent in those phenomena.

If the urge to contribute is, as I propose, a human instinct, then the natural desire to serve others should be present in all people. However, there are a multitude of factors related to ways of thinking, living environments, and so on that cloud the perception of the instinctive urge to contribute, and therefore it often goes unnoticed. Consequently, many fail to act on the urge to contribute in their life mode, and so cannot access the wider perspective it opens on life.

I, too, was once blind to the urge to contribute, but various events that occurred around me awakened my awareness so that it gradually became apparent to me; I began to feel an instinctual urge, a desire to serve others. The events that animated it impressed me at the time as philosophically important and I had a presentiment that they bore directly on the essence of human nature. From that point on I was able to sense a greater depth and breadth in my own existence and in my prospects for the future (as I will describe in more detail in Chapter 3).

It is possible, then, to desire to act altruistically without recognizing that desire as an instinct, but the failure to recognize it as such does not mean that the desire is *not* instinctive.

In any case, I can ask myself: What constitutes 'contributing to the world' in my life mode? I believe that if one can answer this question cogently, based on an understanding of the urge to contribute as an instinct, one's perspective on life reaches a new horizon and important life goals come into sharp focus. This way of thinking does not admit such states of mind as despair or deception, and reflects a clearly defined self. For now it is enough simply to propose that the urge to contribute is an instinct and that it implies an essential truth about human life important enough to consciously activate it in one's chosen life mode. By doing this, one takes a positive, if small, step towards confirming the connection between the premise and conclusion noted at the beginning of this section – if we let the urge to contribute have an effect, our life expands into broader and deeper dimensions.

While acknowledging the importance of words and care in their use, we must avoid becoming lost in abstract wanderings through pure semantics. We need to keep a balance, which requires curiosity about and sensitivity to the way that worldly phenomena reflect things that actually exist, even though we cannot see them. Truth can also be discovered by identifying things that do not exist and thus cannot be seen. This, too, we must remember. In any case, of one thing we can be absolutely certain: to assume that 'what can be seen exists' and that 'what cannot be seen does not exist' will suffocate curiosity and dull our sensitivity to the truth.

How the Contribution Instinct Appears in Verbal Courtesies

One of the most common courtesies in the Japanese language is the phrase *okagesama de*, which translates roughly as 'I am indebted to you (for it)'. This expression reflects the *Homo contribuens* nature of society. In the literal sense, the phrase should be used by the beneficiary of some favour towards the person who bestowed the favour, the benefactor. In reality, however, Japanese speakers use the expression much more freely. Even when A and B meet for the first time if A politely asks, 'Are your parents well?' B will probably reply, 'Okagesama de (Thanks for your kindness)' despite the fact that, having never even met A before, neither B nor B's parents are indebted in the slightest to A.

I know of no corresponding expression in other cultures, at least not in Western cultures. It reflects a singularly Japanese way of thinking. Japanese generally have a deep-rooted sense of their interconnectedness as members of the same society. That is why they often speak of someone's place in society in terms of that person's relations with others. By focusing on those relationships they are expressing an implicit understanding that a person 'living' in society is *being enabled to live* by others, and that recognition circumscribes the idea of the individual living in society.

The use of *okagesama de* even with people we meet for the first time, reflects a general sense of gratitude towards even total strangers for this 'being enabled to live'. The phrase thus expresses the speaker's gratitude to the other both for benefits actually received and for the potential to receive them. The expression of this and similar exchanges vividly illustrates the nature of *Homo contribuens*.

This linking of people through the correlation of living and 'being enabled to live' in society has an intriguing symmetry that suggests ways of exercising the urge to contribute even among total strangers. Insofar as we take the urge to contribute to be an instinct, it is only natural to connect it with anyone, anytime. Furthermore, the sense of living and being enabled to live embodied in *okagesama de* permeates Japanese society, indiscriminate of people's age, social status, occupation, gender, or living environment. Such expressions are thought to be integrally linked with traditional pantheistic beliefs and rituals that required people to show gratitude towards the innumerable deities that abide in all things and by whose grace all things come to be.

This intriguing link between Japanese tradition and the urge to contribute as seen in the phrase *okagesama de* is also strikingly apparent in another uniquely Japanese sentiment known as *mono no aware*. This concept also merits further consideration.

Understanding Mono no Aware

Mono no aware is one of my favourite expressions. Literally meaning 'the pathos of things', it has been variously defined as a heart-felt, often sad appreciation of the world's impermanence, a sensitivity to elegant beauty, a gentle melancholy, and so on. To me, it expresses a poignant emotional response to the phenomena of the external world, including a profound sense of empathy and pathos, pervasive yet serene, towards nature and humanity. The evolving application of the concept in diverse areas of Japanese culture over hundreds of years testifies to the value that Japanese people attach to the sentiment it expresses.

The feeling of *mono no aware* also reflects a dispassionate observation of the world. Nature and human life are in constant flux, subject to myriad changes and unforeseeable events. Life is a finite, single journey through this shifting world. *Mono no aware* is at the heart of a distanced appreciation of the substance of our ephemeral existence.

Countless millions of human beings have lived and died since humanity first appeared on this planet. No one has escaped death. Endless though our dreams of immortality may be, living beings have always been pitifully impotent against the reality of eventual death. The pharaohs of ancient Egypt founded their hopes for immortality on mummification, investing wealth and power into the construction of pyramids to guard their mummies until reincarnation. But though they left behind colossal historical monuments not one of them actually succeeded in coming back to life. The same fate awaited the American business magnate John D. Rockefeller, who declared he would happily give up his entire fortune if he could be cured of illness and outlive the natural span. He died nonetheless, leaving behind immense wealth.

People are born, flourish and fade through the phases of life and eventually pass away. Within that finite, fleeting existence, we have the ability to comprehend the *mono no aware* of things.

Though bound within finitude, this sensibility paradoxically holds a deeper level of permanence that materializes like invisible ink emerging on a blank page.

The advanced technology that has put human beings into outer space and onto the surface of the moon has also opened a unique perspective on the Earth. Viewing our blue planet floating in the vast blackness of space many astronauts have commented on its delicate, fragile existence. The Earth's atmosphere and oceans, which have such an overwhelming presence at ground level, appear to cling precariously to the planet when seen from the moon. Enveloped in that thin mantle of air and water, life on Earth is indeed a precious and fragile thing. In the vast context of universal space ours is a truly ephemeral and tentative existence. It is moving to hear astronauts who have seen the Earth from outer space describe it in terms of ineffable beauty and fragility.

It may seem to be more 'human' to take a passionate rather than a cool, detached view of reality. A display of emotions usually strikes us as the more dynamic response, while dispassionate observation suggests a suppression of real feelings. In fact, this is not the case at all. Quiet contemplation of the world can embrace a profound feeling of *mono no aware*. It is, however, not a prosaic sentiment but a liberated state of mind arising in accordance with the dictates of the untrammelled heart. In order to grasp *mono no aware*, it is essential to suppress the deliberate intensity and passion of the subjective mind and dispel all preconceptions. Viewing things through the lens of self-conscious objectives or rigid preconceptions can distort the facts and as history vividly illustrates, persistent misconceptions can lead to unmitigated disasters.

Religious fundamentalism, for example, involves distortions that, if taken to extremes, can incite terrorism and armed conflict. Systems such as Nazism and communism eventually collapsed from similar extremism. The mentality of fanaticism swells rapidly but it is only a matter of time before it collapses leaving only more scars of regret on the progress of human history.

Conversely, people with concern for and understanding of our tenuous existence are much better fitted to observe nature, human life and human affairs with philosophic calm. All phenomena appear to such minds as pitiably fleeting and mutable, evanescent objects whose essential nature evokes pathos and which are, for that reason, indescribably beautiful and valued.

The integrated whole encompassed in such a broad, dispassionate understanding naturally embraces relations among people, circumstances and environments. They include the Earth's web of ecosystems, all of them finite and limited, within which human existence is no more than a component subsystem.

The Club of Rome has sounded the alert against global population growth and its concomitant strain on resources. It warns that the number of people living on our planet is forecast to reach ten billion in the first half of the twenty-first century while already exceeding its capacity to sustain them. We are well aware that the global population explosion has reached critical proportions, exacerbating poverty and refugee problems worldwide and accelerating the demise of numerous forms of life.

Meanwhile, technological advances have facilitated the manufacture of all kinds of goods and mass production makes them globally available. But not everyone benefits. Some are able to fill their lives with an array of products that was once unimaginable – from processed food and pharmaceuticals to automobiles and electrical appliances – while many others continue to suffer from critical shortages of food and other basic necessities. It is not enough simply to lament this state of affairs. Taking an impartial look at the world's current predicament, we must conclude that contemporary civilization has served the interests of knowledge – more specifically a technologically biased sphere of knowledge – only too well.

In Japanese history the early-modern warlord Oda Nobunaga (1534–82) stands out as a leader who, rejecting convention and received values, applied the perspective of *mono no aware* in pioneering a new epoch. Associating *mono no aware* with Nobunaga, a powerful, militant warlord, may seem incongruous, but this man combined a fine sensitivity to the beauty and pathos in the transience of things with a practised control of the art of calm contemplation of the realities around him.

Nobunaga brought order out of the political chaos that characterized the long twilight of the previous era and forged unity among Japan's warring clans. His achievements, I believe, extended into the modern era, making it possible for Japan to become the nation it is today without ever having to suffer invasion by a foreign power. In my view, Nobunaga's successors, Toyotomi Hideyoshi (1537–98) and Tokugawa Ieyasu (1543–1616), merely carried his work to its completion. Contemporary Japan cannot be fully understood without an appreciation of the role played by Nobunaga, a man who dared to fulfil his lifelong ambition free from the fear of being resented or misunderstood by others.

In his struggle to redress widening incongruities and unjust use of power by the authorities of his day, particularly the provincial military lords and militant Buddhist sects, Nobunaga made it a practice always to coolly scrutinize the situation before taking action. He was willing to risk criticism and severe challenges in order to eradicate the outmoded values held by those in authority. I suspect that behind his ambition and ability lay a profound sense of *mono no aware* and an intensely strong urge to contribute to a better world for future generations.

The reality is that each of us moves ineluctably and knowingly towards his/her own death as an entirely finite being. It was with this sense of *mono no aware* that I intuited the existence of the urge to contribute. We should seek strength in the spirit of *mono no aware*. Far from a feeble and ineffectual sentiment, like Pascal's 'thinking reed' it has a supple potency backed by delicate sensibility and force.

Chance Encounters and Gratitude

I enjoy interacting with other people regardless of their background or social position. I try to approach people without preconceptions or prejudice no matter who they are and am eager to experience new encounters whenever possible. This inclination is a facet of my being, an instinctive reaction to the world.

Each of us can meet only a finite number of people over the course of a lifetime, and for me each encounter has the potential to bring immeasurable joy. I believe that one of the most important tasks of my life is to try to realize that potential and because I see encounters with new people in this way I feel a deep sense of gratitude each time they occur.

When meeting someone for the first time, we may occasionally feel offended by something the other person says. There are people who notice only the shortcomings of new acquaintances and therefore expect little from subsequent encounters. For me, however, the joy of meeting new people is to identify their virtues and that joy remains undiminished, even if they lack experience or have shortcomings. In encounters of the most uneventful kind – a silent exchange of bows with an elderly stranger I pass on the street, for example – I experience an emotional upsurge that is difficult to describe. I suspect it is the same for many people.

When I have the opportunity to speak with people I have just met I try to be wholly attentive to what they have to say. Often a casual remark made by my interlocutor inspires in me a striking, imaginative response. To experience these vivid images arising out of an unexpected fragment of speech is another welcome consequence of the other's presence. Meeting people is, to me, the spice of life, an experience that affords an indefinable benefit. That is why I always try to have an open, unprejudiced attitude towards the people I meet and to carefully consider everything they say.

Perhaps some mediating force is at work in such encounters whose nature can be divined only by experience. And once people realize that such occasions can be deeply affective, perhaps they will learn to approach everyone they meet without preconceptions or prejudice.

Referring to the way people come into contact with one another literary critic Katsuichiro Kamei (1907–66) defined the chance encounter as, 'the occasion of a blood bond between history, current social reality and the individual'. Also thought-provoking in this regard is the view of history he expresses in the following passage:

> No matter how detailed our knowledge of events and people of the past, we cannot say we truly understand history by such knowledge alone. History is the vast enormity of human life. It is only when one happens to meet this or that person and responds to him as a living, flesh-and-blood person, as teacher or friend, that history becomes a living thing. History in this sense is the occasion of the interaction of life with life. We draw life from encounters with our unknown ancestors.
>
> (Katsuichiro Kamei, *Ai no mujo ni tsuite* [On the Transience of Love], Kodansha, 1971)

I mention chance encounters and gratitude in this context because I feel the urge to contribute only in interaction with other people and because my understanding of it as an instinct has been corroborated many times through such contact. As long as one has the urge to contribute a sense of gratitude should arise spontaneously at the moment of such contact and if one channels that feeling properly, the urge to contribute flows forth from it like a spring.

Episode 2
Love Suppressed

The restaurant I was looking for was tucked away in a secluded corner of Yokohama's Chinatown, off to the left from the main street leading to the

Zenrinmon gate. The wooden door-frame was decorated with a jewel-inlaid, rising-dragon carving. The restaurant's interior was larger than one expected from the outside. In the rear were a number of round tables partitioned off by a folding screen on which was depicted a boy shouldering a Chinese zither.

Just as our dinner party was getting into full swing I noticed another group who had taken the table next to us. Among them, behind the folding screen, was a woman wearing a black shawl, who for some reason attracted my interest. As I sipped my Chinese tea I kept glancing in her direction. Then it occurred to me that the faint perfume that had begun to drift across to me was probably coming from the woman's shawl. At the same time I noticed she was wearing only one silver earring, the right one. Neither the woman herself nor anyone around her seemed to have noticed that the left one was missing. The delicate fragrance smelled something like fennel, though at that distance the aroma was not very strong. My thoughts strayed to the missing earring: I suspected it had fallen either onto the table top or onto the floor.

A moment later my eye was caught by a shiny glint beside the leg of the woman's chair, it was the missing earring. Naturally I should have stood up and spoken to her, but for some reason I could not. While I sat there in silent hesitation, the woman herself finally noticed the earring and, still seated, reached down to pick it up. At that point I could have stood and picked it up for her and I thought I should, but somehow I just could not bring myself to rise from my seat.

The woman gently extended her fingers towards the floor. Even from where I was, some distance away, I saw the controlled flurry of her five lean fingers as they stretched for the earring. A subtle blue pattern of veins glowed from within her pale, svelte hand and as the outstretched middle finger curved into a bow the nail at its tip gleamed pearly white. I held in check a feeling of love that I would neither reveal nor act upon.

CHAPTER 3

LIBERATION FROM NIHILISM

ℭ

*When people are freed from the nihilism that pain and death
can engender they see new possibilities and experience a
spontaneous urge to contribute something to the world.*

A New Attitude to Posterity

In this chapter I want to review the process that carried me through my own experience of nihilism and then sense of purpose that led me, while discovering how those ideas are connected with the urge to contribute, to the realization that the urge to contribute is a human instinct innate to everyone.

After my philosophical awakening at Takeshi's death, I passed the remainder of my school and university years haunted by a vague sense of the vanity and transience of our existence. Even so, I was also beginning to glean, albeit dimly, something of the potent joy that can be derived from responding to a keen sense of purpose for the benefit of other people. I was, nonetheless, still ten years away from formulating the idea that an instinctive urge to contribute lay behind such joy. At that point, then, the reality of the urge to contribute as a universal instinct was still, for me, a truth that existed but was unrecognized.

As a young man I thought the joy I found in doing things for others was a feeling peculiar to me, not present in the nature of human beings in general. At the same time, it bothered me that I could not deduce from where the desire to act altruistically could possibly come. The question preoccupied me, like someone searching for fish in a winter lake covered with thin ice, I felt sure the answer was somewhere near, just below the surface.

My encounter with philosophical problems when I was in my early teens stirred in me an interest in questions about human nature that was slightly unusual for my age. As I learned more about how Takeshi had pursued his studies right to the last I gradually formulated a rough picture of his state of mind at that time. This avenue of thought led me for the first time to the concept and reality underlying the term 'sense of purpose'. I began to think that if people have a compelling sense of purpose or mission and respond to it, they can approach life in a forward-looking, positive way right up to the moment of death.

Then, when I was about twenty-five, I came across the following maxim whose impact propelled me towards another important step in my philosophical development: 'In relation to future generations people have responsibilities, not rights; in relation to past generations people have rights, not responsibilities'. I interpret this to mean that each of us lives surrounded by other people; each of us in society is connected to people who are affected by what we think and do – dependent family members, for example, or workplace subordinates – as well as to people whose opinions substantially affect our own life, such as elders, benefactors and workplace superiors. Bearing in mind these two kinds of interpersonal relations, I tried restating the maxim this way: In relation to people whose lives one affects one has responsibilities, not rights, and in relation to people who affect one's own life one has rights, not responsibilities. Using this interpretation, I could see with growing clarity the cogent idea of the role of a 'sense of purpose' as the impetus for fulfilling one's responsibilities towards those whose lives one affects.

If I could think of people whose lives I affect as my 'personal posterity', then that aphorism taught me that each of us has the mission of protecting those who are our personal posterity and that all humans have what I am calling a natural 'sense of purpose' that anchors and guides our awareness of that mission. This was the moment when the reality of the human sense of purpose became clearly apparent to me in all its dimensions.

Curiously, with this awakening the nihilistic mood that had troubled me since Takeshi's death completely evaporated. What remained was simply the feeling that I must cherish and protect my posterity as I cherish and protect my own life, leading to the belief that this attitude generates all the necessary meaning for life. With this philosophical step, I was liberated from my abiding doubts about the ultimate meaninglessness of life.

In my conception of our natural sense of purpose, I saw my responsibilities as extending impartially to all who belong to my posterity: no matter how malicious other people might be, as long as they are among those whose lives I influence, I must do everything possible to protect them all equally. Thinking about it from another perspective, perhaps this idea of an all-embracing responsibility to my 'posterity', including those I might consider malicious or dishonest, contrived to expunge nihilistic thoughts from my mind and invest 'sense of purpose' with its true meaning.

Consequently, this idea became a reference point around which I finally gained some understanding of why Socrates willingly drank his poison.

By thus identifying my own modest mission in life, I found that I had achieved a firmly grounded sense of contentment. The idea that this mission applied to all other people whose lives I affected suggested to me an instinct intrinsic to human nature. It would be some time, however, before I linked that instinct to the concept of an innate urge to contribute.

Discovery of the Urge to Contribute

Only when approaching my late thirties did the urge to contribute – until then a reality that existed though I could not see it – begin gradually to assume some form in my mind, revitalizing my interest in philosophy.

Around that time, I was diagnosed with a certain bone disorder. I knew that there were various kinds of bone disease but as I listened to the doctor my first thought was that I had bone marrow cancer. Two weeks later, however, the results of my tests came back and I was told that I had a rare condition known as a giant cell tumour.

This condition develops in three stages with some variation depending on the factors causing the abnormality. In the first stage, the condition can be completely cured by surgically removing the affected area. From the second stage on, however, even after removal of one tumour the disease may recur and spread to the pelvis or some other part of the body. In the third stage, the disease may continue to spread to multiple sites even after surgery and can lead to bone marrow cancer. I was diagnosed with a second-stage giant cell tumour. It was incised and, presumably because the surgery was successful, I have since had no reason to suspect any recurrence.

During the period of my diagnosis and treatment, however, even some slight pain in the bones of my legs precipitated a grim presentiment of death. I had learned, furthermore, that pain control becomes very difficult once this disease reaches an advanced stage, and in the incidence of bone marrow cancer, within six months the intensity of pain goes beyond the limits of the morphine-based pain relief available at the time.

Under the duress of acute physical pain human beings become almost powerless. Pain is entirely self-specific; other people can perceive the signs of my pain but they cannot share it any more than I can turn away from it.

Aiming for the core
– based on the sculpture *The Poseidon of Artemision*. If we take our enquiry to the very core of human nature, to the point where no further explanation is possible, we find there the *a priori* urge to contribute – which I envision as being apprehended by a calm, level gaze that hits upon the truth.

To feel intense pain challenges one's sense of one's own reality and that kind of pain can confound even the firmest resolve. The victim of pain, whose torment no one else can feel, may respond in various ways – with solitary fortitude and self-control, sometimes with courage, sometimes with self-indulgence and often with an urgent desire to do something while there is still time. I felt frustrated at the thought that I could not communicate the reality of true pain to anyone else.

Until my diagnosis was confirmed, my faith in the idea that a sense of purpose enables one to live with a positive attitude right to the point of death was beginning to waver. The thought that I may be subjected to excruciating pain was terrifying. At times my distress was so great that I almost convinced myself that it would be better to end things quickly with a pistol than have my whole philosophy of life distorted by prolonged pain.

As a storm of such thoughts raged in my mind I felt I was gaining a suggestion, this time through firsthand experience, of the feelings of people who know they are nearing the end of their lives. At the same time, I had to deal with the conflict between my philosophy of death in general and the ineluctable reality of my own death. Fortunately, I received good treatment at an early stage and the condition was arrested before it developed into invasive bone marrow disease. I was spared the truly tormenting pain that would have ensued.

I am convinced that this experience, which in some ways resembles being diagnosed with terminal cancer, raised my awareness to certain truths that until then had been invisible. These things became clear to me just as I began to doubt my idea about mission, that a sense of purpose is the key to a positive attitude that prevails even to the time of death. Also at that moment I was suffused with a desire to use what little time I had left for the benefit of posterity. Until then I had only dimly sighted the urge to contribute away in the distance but now it was beginning to advance and acquire a closer and sharper focus in my mind. Given my potentially grave medical condition it seemed clear that to act for posterity's sake was the optimum way to make my life useful and meaningful.

Other feelings began to stir in my heart. My mind became filled with recollections of people, ideas and words I had encountered up to that point in my life and I realized how immeasurably important all those other people were in my life. I remembered something vital: for all the years I had lived, my life depended on the consideration and grace of other people. That memory took shape in my mind as the concept I call the urge to contribute.

At that point, I decided to keep a scrupulous record of the pain I was experiencing in my diseased bones. I might have been hoping that a detailed, first-hand record of pain as only the sufferer could know it would in some small way advance medical knowledge and treatment of this condition. Whatever the reason, I wanted to throw myself into something more than an abstract, lofty ideal. I wanted to express my sense of purpose in an activity that felt natural and spontaneous. At what I thought might be the final stage of my life I was filled with a consuming urge to be of service to other people.

In my case I did not make a detour into hedonism before experiencing this spontaneous desire to contribute to some greater good, it arose quickly and I soon found particular joy in two things: one was the realization that I could be of service to others even from my sick bed. The other was my discovery that as soon as I did something for someone else, even in such circumstances, I was freed from my fear of death.

Some time later, I met Ikuo Hirayama (b. 1930), the pre-eminent Japanese-style painter and president of Tokyo University of Fine Arts and Music. It was humbling to hear the story of Hirayama's response to a similar experience. He had forged on with his artistic activities even after developing leukaemia (the result of radiation exposure from the atomic bombing of Hiroshima) and in spite of the severe fatigue caused by the disease. Hirayama wrote of his personal struggle in what I consider a masterpiece, *Bukkyo denrai* (The Coming of Buddhism; Kodansha, 2 vols., 1991/05). The work was inspired by the famous story of Xuan-zang (known in Japan as Genjo Sanzo-hoshi), the seventh-century Chinese monk who travelled for years through India and the neighbouring regions collecting Buddhist teachings to bring back to China. In his book *Michi haruka* (The Road Afar; Nihon Keizai Shimbunsha, 1991), Hirayama writes that painting 'is ultimately something the artist accomplishes not by skill or technique as much as something transcending the self'. He talks about how, after reading an article in 1964 about the Olympic flame being carried to Japan via the Silk Road, he was inspired to create some truly monumental paintings related to the spread of Buddhism. Since then he has produced numerous works on that theme.

I am fortunate to enjoy an ongoing friendship with Ikuo Hirayama and have drawn many valuable lessons from the unflagging vigour with which he participates in life. If people can find meaning in their own existence and fulfilment in their imme-diate lives and circumstances, even in adversity, they can lead full and forward-looking lives. By pursuing his art and life in his chosen way, Ikuo Hirayama has achieved this in exemplary fashion.

At the risk of exploiting another's achievements to promote my own propositions, I believe Hirayama was motivated by what I regard as an innate sense of purpose and urge to contribute, expressed, in his case, through art. His irrepressible urge to make a contribution to the world of art engendered a consciousness of mission, which in turn naturally gave rise to an experience of artistic fulfilment so strong that it could suppress his illness.

The A Priori *Urge to Contribute*

Insofar as they come at the critical, final stages of life, the issues that arise in the minds of people with terminal or life-threatening

Deep contemplation
– based on a sailboat depicted on an Archaic-period wine cup. Neither
my feelings nor my body can step beyond the bounds of my skin.
Only speculative thought can serve as a sailboat bound for truth,
bearing me slowly beyond the self towards the only true answer.

diseases, such as advanced cancer, leave no room for compromise. The same kind of uncompromising compulsion seized me during my illness, propelling me towards some mission. It made me realize that the intense sense of purpose I experienced then might spring from an instinct and that led me to the notion of an instinctive urge to contribute. I became convinced that other phenomena in human experience could also be explained by understanding that the desire to contribute to the world arises from instinct.

People feel a desire to do something for others at other times also, not just when they are very ill or dying. Consider, for example, the experiences of Kim Dae Jung (b. 1925), former president of the Republic of Korea (South Korea) and winner of the Nobel Peace Prize in 2000 for his work to promote reconciliation and peace between his country and the Democratic People's Republic of Korea (North Korea). During the Korean War, Kim was captured by enemy troops and only narrowly escaped execution as his North Korean captors withdrew before a US and South Korean advance. I was moved to hear Kim recount how this fortuitous second chance of life kindled in him a fervent desire to be of service to the Korean people. This was another instance when a strong sense of mission arose out of a life-threatening crisis, giving natural expression to an instinctive urge to contribute to the greater good.

The need to serve and the mission people feel at certain times seemed to operate in much the same way as inspiration, arising in a sudden flash and for no apparent reason, often shows us the right course of action; or the way a precise auxiliary line can elucidate the solution to a knotty problem of geometry. With the same kind of certainty, all of my philosophical musings now coalesced into a coherent whole. Furthermore, once I had concluded that the will to contribute must be an instinct I became increasingly aware of how many phenomena in human life and society were amenable to explanation in these terms.

Perhaps, I thought, there is a natural instinct which arises in the human heart when it is disencumbered of a nihilistic attitude towards death and which inspires us to be of service to other people. Moreover, if it is possible to feel a sense of mission firm enough to stake one's life on, then it seems natural to conclude that the urge to contribute is an instinct in human beings.

On the other hand, if all people have this innate urge to contribute – this built-in instinct to act in the interests of others – then why do disputes and conflicts arise? Insofar as we regard the urge to contribute as deriving from instinct we must go back to the ontological categories mentioned earlier in this book, namely, 'that which exists even though it is not perceived' and 'that which does not exist and therefore is not perceived'. Let me clarify my meaning.

The human sense of mission does not always subdue the instinct for pleasure. We cannot expect everyone to be like Socrates or to spend his or her last months of life in study as Takeshi did. The important thing is that the same invisible element of human nature exists just as surely in people who take the path of hedonism as in those who act upon the more altruistic sense of mission. That is, when the sense of mission is not acted upon it is not because it is non-existent and thus cannot be perceived, rather, it exists but is not perceived and the failure to perceive it precludes the likelihood that it will be acted upon or applied in practice.

The same can be said of the urge to contribute. In supposing the urge to contribute to be an instinct, my premise is that it is an *a priori* (innate) impulse. Under the influence of other forces, however, this instinctive impulse may be distorted or redirected, creating psychological conflict and frustration and sometimes unleashing a spiritual energy operating in direct opposition to any intention to contribute to the greater good. Even then, however, the urge to contribute is still an instinct present and active in the depths of the human heart, existing unrecognized and unmanifested not because it is not there but even though it is there.

Furthermore, when the urge to contribute is manifested in an overt desire to serve others, the true motive for action is not based on any particular sense of what others need. Although that may be one factor, a specific awareness of others' needs is preceded by one's own initial impulse, one's personal need, simply to do something for other people. That means that the altruist seeks to act upon the urge to contribute essentially for his or her own sake. The urge to contribute is thus not a selfless intention as much as it is a kind of self-assertion rooted in instinct.

Humans are social beings. If we recast the inclination to be of service along with the ways it comes into play, in terms of the new perspective of instinct, then we have to consider not only individual states of mind but also broader social issues from the same viewpoint. In that endeavour, which I consider a philosophical one, the concept of the urge to contribute can serve as a kind of auxiliary line drawn by reason in the contemplative mind to help solve problems both in an individual life and in our increasingly directionless contemporary society.

Volunteerism and the Urge to Contribute

The terms volunteerism and volunteer activities are somewhat in vogue these days but they are not often clearly defined. What categories of activity does volunteerism cover? The following is from a *Yomiuri shimbun* newspaper article that sought to identify the boundary between volunteer activities and activities of a private, personal nature.

> No one would call taking care of your aging parent in your own home a 'volunteer activity'. But what about informally checking on the elderly woman who lives next door, or helping at a nursing

home caring for people you've never met before? The line of demarcation between volunteer activities and other kinds of activity is not easy to draw.

Concerning environmental protection it is just as difficult to make a clear distinction between local community issues and problems that are national in scale.

Taking part in environmental protection activities in one's own local area certainly counts as volunteer work but in some respects it is the same kind of task as looking after one's own aging parents. We cannot expect others to protect the natural environment of our own community; if we don't do it ourselves no one will.

The people who value their community and are most familiar with it are spontaneously willing to participate in its improvement. To them this is not a volunteer activity or community service.

In the United States there is an attitude nicknamed NIMBY, an acronym for 'Not in my back yard'. It would seem at first to represent an ordinary, selfless kind of environmental protectionism for the community but it can also be just another form of selfishness. (*Yomiuri shimbun*, 10 November 1999)

This article makes the point that a great many people are in fact involved in volunteer activities of some sort, even in the absence of a clear-cut definition of the term. Often we cannot clearly distinguish where the sphere of private, personal life ends and that of volunteer work begins. Activities aimed at protecting the local environment or other interests of one's own community serve the general good in some sense but they also stem from more selfish, narrow, NIMBY-type concerns. Considered in that light what might have been seen as selflessness in the volunteerism that I believe stems from the urge to contribute suddenly seems, in many cases, to transmute into a kind of egoism. That may, in fact, be exactly what it is.

Despite the difficulty of formulating a clear definition of volunteerism I would like to use the *Yomiuri* article to discuss how we can differentiate between selfless efforts to serve the greater good and self-centred endeavours that serve oneself.

This area of debate began with the observation that few people would regard taking care of their elderly parent as a volunteer activity. In general, we do not consider family members under our care as being the beneficiaries of volunteer work. What about the elderly woman next door whom we look in on and talk with from time to time? Some might say this activity counts as volunteerism or community service because the woman is not family. Others, however, may feel that a neighbour is still too close to be regarded as someone for whom we are doing volunteer work, or that merely chatting with someone does not qualify as such an act.

In my view, offering kind words and conversation to elderly people, whoever they are, is an important expression of the spirit of contribution. It is from such casual, everyday courtesies that many elderly people derive both vitality and peace of mind. By the same token, I believe even practical nursing care cannot truly ease the elderly, either in body or mind, unless it is provided in a sincerely caring spirit. Accordingly, I regard the purposeful act of conversing with and checking on an unrelated elderly neighbour to be a *bone fide* volunteer act.

Some people may point out that the selfless spirit behind the act in this case would not normally qualify it as volunteerism. On the other hand, unpaid work in a nursing home would almost always be clearly considered a volunteer activity. This is because elderly people at a nursing home are further removed from the volunteer's daily life – his or her personal realm – than the elderly person who lives next door. It is a matter of social distance, or degree of 'otherness'. Because we tend to think of volunteerism primarily in terms of acting – without conditions of material rewards – in the interests of 'others', the more distant the other person the more nearly the activity fits our image of volunteer work. We also associate hands-on nursing care and other practical, visible types of work with volunteerism more than we do social interchange or just human contact. Nursing care is clearly considered different from neighbourly greetings, which is customary, everyday behaviour that anyone can and is expected to exhibit. In sum, most of us definitely have preconceptions about volunteerism, particularly the notion that volunteer activities are generally directed at benefiting people situated at a certain social distance from oneself.

If, then, we consider the volunteer's distance from the beneficiary and the nature of the service performed, we begin to form a coherent concept of those services performed without pay for certain other people and for the wider community that we have been calling volunteer activities. This category of behaviour spans a wide spectrum, including care of the sick, elderly and disabled, disaster relief, food aid, philanthropy of various kinds and general environmentalism.

The newspaper article quoted earlier notes the difficulty of distinguishing local community issues from those of national importance and makes the challenging proposal that while performing services in support of the environment or public welfare in one's own community qualifies as volunteer work, that kind of activity is fundamentally the same type of task as taking care of one's own aging parents.

If at this point we propose that a local community exists not just for individuals but also has a wider significance for many others, then the debate takes on a new dimension. We can still regard the community as belonging exclusively to those who live there, or we can view it as belonging to 'others' or to 'everyone', thereby establishing a certain degree of separation between the individual who lives there and that community. If we take the latter perspective, then, by our definition, we can regard activities performed within one's own community as a type of volunteer work.

That point of view allows participants in even the most highly localized, community-specific activities to regard those activities as being of wider relevance. What they do in the community is not exclusively their own affair. The community belongs neither to individuals nor to people living elsewhere. As the smallest unit of regional society, a community is often regarded as 'belonging' to the people who live in it. However, the concept of a collective 'we' as a small social unit arises in the first place from a consciousness that transcends the individual self. Therefore the idea of service to the community sometimes extends to situations that involve 'others', and the interests of the few must be subsidiary to broader collective interests.

In other words, we are expected to exercise our natural and instinctive urge to contribute to the local community and the wider society that is 'ours' and this requires us to reach beyond the bounds of personal or familial concerns. I suspect that the roots of the spirit of volunteerism lie in that sense of going beyond self and family to serve others.

In any case, how one regards unpaid service for the benefit of one's own community varies according to the way one conceives the public arena. In my view, people who give of their time and expertise spontaneously, that is, from the urge to contribute as an instinct or as the 'fifth life mode', do so out of genuine concern for their community. That concern leads them to spontaneous action in the interests of others. Insofar as this is an urge arising from instinct, it is necessarily a matter of the self, but it cannot be considered selfishness.

Philanthropy

Here I use the word philanthropy to describe the activities of non-profit and non-governmental organizations, which have been rapidly proliferating in the last decade or so. The term itself is a compound of the Greek roots *phil* (love) and *anthropo* (human beings) and so 'philanthropy' literally means 'love of humanity'.

Certainly, it is from love that the spirit of contributing is born and activities in service to others are a manifestation of love. But there are many kinds of love. Affection is a kind of love that suppresses the self and gives rise to the urge to contribute, which is expressed in concrete acts of kindness and helping. Another kind of love is based on sympathy and we feel it as pity or compassion. This type of love also draws out the urge to contribute, which manifests itself in specific actions.

Normally, we do not distinguish between different kinds of acts that contribute to society according to whether they arise from love or compassion or some other feeling. Sometimes, however, pity contains condescension, the tacit assumption of superiority, and it may involve a subtle displacement of genuine sympathy by pride or vanity. Although pride and vanity may in practice provide powerful impetus towards benevolence, the acts arising from such sentiments are not the products of the urge to contribute. Pride and vanity are instances of feelings directed towards oneself, which is in diametric opposition to the essential quality of the urge to contribute.

Thus, while they are ostensibly similar, constructive types of behaviour such as aid-giving, care-giving and making donations, spring from a variety of impulses. As long as it benefits the recipients, however, all benevolent activity contributes to the broader social good.

In many situations benevolent acts prompted by pride or vanity have a greater impact than those inspired by affection or love. For example, some people make enormous donations to charity simply to flaunt their involvement in philanthropic causes and in so doing do a lot of good for others.

In short, benevolent activity is effective regardless of the sentiments behind it. From the standpoint of practical effect, even pride and vanity contribute to the greater social good when they inspire benevolent acts. However, benevolent acts inspired by excessive pity or compassion can sometimes be offensive. Even though acts done out of questionable sentiments are good in themselves and are a way to contribute, their inspiration and purpose show that they are not products of the urge to contribute.

Delight in giving is essentially instinctive and all forms of benevolence are fundamentally products of natural feelings. As long as acts of benevolence are rooted in love, the beneficiaries also can feel genuine joy. A simple, unaffected desire to contribute that stems from love and reflects that person's genuine feeling towards others is what I mean by the instinctive urge to contribute.

The human heart is naturally a complex of feelings, never at rest with a single sentiment, be it affection, pity, pride or vanity. Essentially, our inner being is a composite of subtly interwoven emotions. But when the self is concerned only with itself, as in pride or vanity, it cannot manifest the ineffable ability we all have, through the urge to contribute, to make concern for others also serve the interests of the self.

The Urge to Contribute: Cultural Differences between East and West

I would like to offer some personal observations about instincts, treating them as innate capacities governed by laws of nature and noting some differences in the way they are perceived in Eastern and Western cultures.

At the risk of oversimplifying, perhaps we can say that in the Christian worldview underlying Western culture, people are regarded, in part, as God's servants. The desire to serve others is understood in similar terms, the ultimate contribution being to carry out the will of God. The desire to serve others is more or less identified with the desire to serve God and as such is associated with selflessness and noble virtue. In such a cultural milieu it is not difficult to explain why volunteerism, community service, civic duty – all of which are expressions of what is a spontaneous inclination to contribute to society – are included in the curriculum of many schools in the West.

Conversely, the realm where natural laws operate tends increasingly to be regarded as the domain of the natural sciences. Human instinct, for example, is more and more widely understood entirely in physiological terms, not spiritual. More than ever, the mechanisms of the mind and spirit are seen as functions of the brain, the body's endocrine system, and so on. For this reason, causal theories developed in the natural sciences have often clashed in the West with the teleology of Christian belief. A prime example is the furore over the theory of evolution. Not until the last few years of the twentieth century was any serious progress made to reconcile aspects of evolutionism and conservative Christian teleology and the conflict between them is far from over.

In the past, human beings developed the technologies that became the foundation of industrial society by applying scientific theory derived from the observation of natural laws acting on matter and they could see themselves as striving in the service of God.

In that sense, the development of technology has been ends-oriented. Even business and marketing, areas in which I myself have long been involved, still carry vestiges of ties to traditional Western teleology, for example in expressions like the 'invisible hand (of God)' in market theory.

In the intellectual traditions of the East, including Japan, Korea, China and India, we find the cultural influence of Buddhism. In my view, this Eastern, largely Buddhist outlook is concerned mainly with causes and effects rather than with ultimate ends. In this milieu ends-oriented behaviour is subsumed into and controlled by the law of karmic cause and effect. This outlook is highly suggestive of animism wherein all things in nature are believed to possess spirit and nature in all its manifestations is identified with divine beings. The Eastern world does not have a native counterpart to the Western dualism that places matter and phenomena in one dimension and mind and spirit in another. Accordingly, in the Japanese and other Eastern traditions it is normal to regard feelings like the urge to contribute as part of human instinct, in contrast with the common Western understanding of instinct as limited to bodily urges. I have tried to accommodate these differences between Eastern and Western perceptions by distinguishing between physiological and psychological instincts and characterizing the urge to contribute as belonging to the latter category.

Episode 3
Cancer and Hydrangeas

The moment the metal tube pierced the periosteum (the membrane covering the bone) was so painful I thought the local anaesthetic must not have worked. A test sample of bone was extracted from my ailing knee and whisked away to the pathology lab.

It was early in the summer of 1976 when what I thought was a torn muscle in my knee was diagnosed as a bone disease. With the x-rays of my knee still up on the viewer and other doctors also present, the rheumatism specialist – trying to be as cheerful as he could – said only this: 'For the time being it's probably best for you to check into the hospital.' Out in the bright noonday sun moments later I felt the constricting tension inside me suddenly slacken.

As I left the hospital the steamy air rising from the pavement under the early summer sun was stifling. The confusion of the town, the clamour of traffic, everything added to the discomfort of the heat. Shielding my now officially diseased knee, I walked on slowly, but certain at least of my destination. I was headed for the nearest bookstore to find material on the treatment of bone cancer.

As I passed a small, inner-city park along the way I noticed a bed of hydrangeas surrounded by *keyaki* (zelkova trees). The flowers were wilting and had lost most of their colour, though faint traces of blue remained on some of the wispy petals. Sunlight through the trees sprinkled a deserted sandbox with dappled shade.

It was a familiar scene of an ordinary park, but as I gazed around at the plants and objects in it my eyes kept returning to the wilted hydrangeas – they seemed to be telling me that I myself would one day wither and fade like them. The sun's glare was torture, I wanted to hide and languish a while in the shade of one of the large *keyaki* trees. But I could not turn my back on reality, not with so many employees depending on me. If my bone condition did turn out to be cancer, pain control treatments would start to be ineffective in about six months. I had many things to accomplish in that short time.

After buying all the books on bone cancer I could find in the bookstore I went straight to the office and called a meeting of all the department heads in my company. During the meeting I felt as though I were talking with my staff in one voice while holding a dialogue with myself in another; if the pain was going to become unbearable sooner or later, I told myself, then I would be better off committing suicide. At that moment, I realized with a start that I had entered a state of mind unthinkable under normal circumstances free from the thought of death.

Normally, when considering the tasks I face in my work and life, the possibility of failure occurs to me at least once. On that day, however, I found myself in an extremely optimistic frame of mind, I thought of all the things I could do if I did not have cancer and of how splendidly I could develop the land my predecessors had purchased for development if only I could live for another ten years. To me, as I contemplated what could be done, the possibility of failure seemed totally irrelevant.

CHAPTER 4

BEYOND OBLIGATION,
HIGHER THAN DUTY

ൟ

Strip human nature to its core, to the fundamental
elements from which nothing more can be pared away
and there you will find the urge to contribute.

Non-profit Activities and the Self-fulfilment of Instinct

Management guru Peter Drucker has predicted that the twenty-first century will be characterized by, among other things, proliferating non-profit organizations (NPOs), which will comprise a key growth sector and robust growth of non-governmental organizations (NGOs), in particular (Peter Drucker, *Peter Drucker on the Profession of Management*, Harvard Business School Press, 1998). True to his prediction non-profit activity does appear to be on the rise worldwide, while the emergence of this sector as a significant force is bringing various problems into focus. As more and more people become involved in non-profit and volunteer organizations, criticism of political leadership and of the international community is growing stronger and more vocal, raising issues that demand attention.

My concern here is not with legitimate criticism of political or economic affairs, nor do I mean to be alarmist about the expansion of non-profit organizations and activities; but there seems to be an underlying assumption in this sector that 'quantity is strength' and therefore any kind of contribution to and by such organizations is good. Once this attitude starts to crystallize into criticism of anything and everything that might constrain non-profit activities, it deteriorates into the pressurized imposition of values upon others. In conventional thinking non-profit and volunteer activities are regarded as virtuous because they spring from good intentions rather than the hope for material gain. This established view provides no theoretical basis on which to counter the imposition of values. We need a new standard by which to rethink the assumptions 'quantity is strength' and 'contribution is a virtue' underlie the burgeoning non-profit sector.

Let us revisit the idea that the urge to contribute is an instinct and apply it, like an auxiliary line, to the 'problem' of the nature of non-profit and volunteer activities. We thus find that to make a contribution in whatever form cannot possibly be a 'virtue' because, according to our way of thinking, altruistic activities, including nonprofit and volunteer work, are undertaken ultimately for the satisfaction of the performer. From our point of view all altruistic/contributing behaviour, although directed towards others, is seated entirely in one's own instinct and based subjectively on one's own values.

Although a number of NPOs and NGOs raise issues concerning the way the international community is managed and criticize the status quo, many of their criticisms are irrelevant. According to my thesis, altruistic activities must proceed from a clear understanding that all such behaviour springs from the performer's instinct and is therefore undertaken for the performer's sake, otherwise, many well-intentioned projects will ultimately collapse under the weight of self-contradiction. At least, that is the likely outcome if we rely on conventional philosophical approaches to appraise the issues raised by nonprofit activities.

Recently, NGO-based and other activities have been incurring criticism for ignoring the specific needs of the region or community they target, resulting in loss of control over the projects they were detailed to complete. This is another instance where the idea of the urge to contribute as instinct offers a solution.

Before considering specific local needs, the nonprofit performer who responds to the urge to contribute does so to satisfy an instinctive desire to be of service to others. The motivation for the altruistic act lies in the performer's instinct and precedes any consideration of what the intended beneficiary actually wants.

On the other hand, the intended beneficiary, the one directly affected by the particular crisis at hand, thinks first of all about whether or not the services provided give due consideration to what is genuinely needed in their particular case. If, in the view of the beneficiary they do not, then the activities being undertaken are not only worthless they could also be detrimental to the beneficiary. In certain circumstances, such 'services' are regarded as imposed, unwanted charity.

The desire to act for the benefit of others flows from an imperative instinct that compels one to act upon the urge to contribute. Accordingly, if the behaviour inspired by this urge is criticized for, say, overlooking local needs, then the aspiring altruists involved should be able to accept that reproach with humility once they truly appreciate the nature of their own motivation – that is, once they understand it as embedded in their own instinct.

I suggest that this view of the urge to contribute as instinct is applicable to all types of nonprofit/volunteer activity. Of course, the blind, reckless aspects of this instinct should be prevented from becoming too elevated. With incisive self-awareness of his motives the altruist can at least accept with humility the comments and criticisms others may have about his well-intentioned behaviour, thus making it possible to avert any imposition of values by the altruist. In short, the altruist must be aware and act on a genuine urge to contribute, recognizing that urge as an instinct operating in his own self-interest, he can then accept graciously the critiques of those whose interests he aims to serve.

Making a Contribution: An Obligation or a Right?

In understanding the urge to contribute to be an instinct, I believe acting upon that urge to be something akin to a right. Just as the pursuit of health is a fundamental human right, so the fulfilment of basic instincts is a necessary condition of life and is also a right.

From the same standpoint, if I were asked whose obligation it is to help me exercise my right to pursue good health and satisfy my urge to contribute I would say it is mine. To go on living a healthy, wholesome life is an obligation I have towards the life I have been given. Thus, my right to act upon the urge to contribute arises in relation to this obligation to myself. Normally, relationships involving rights and duties or rights and obligations are between one person and another but here the relationship operates within the same individual. Moreover, in the case of the urge to contribute, the indicator pointing towards the object of that urge often points in the direction opposite from that anticipated.

Consider the example of caring for one's aged parents. This is generally considered to be an obligation but if we proceed from the premise that the urge to contribute is an instinct, the right/obligation configuration is turned on its head; sons and daughters have the *right* to care for their parents. This position can be expressed thus: nothing is more pleasing for sons and daughters than to please their parents and that includes taking care of them in their old age. By so doing the children are also commended by others. To experience these joys can therefore be regarded as a son's or daughter's right. This peculiar new way of thinking makes the performance of good deeds for others the privilege, not the duty, of the performer.

Rights and obligations are normally intertwined; a right entails a corresponding obligation and vice versa. An obligation from one person involves a right of another. Rights and obligations can thus be seen in terms of self-other relationships and self-other relationships often entail rights and obligations.

The recipient of an act performed out of a sense of obligation usually feels a sense of right in regard to that act. The reverse is also true. In such cases of acts performed by one person for another, the performer and the recipient can be differentiated according to rights and obligations. Yet there are acts in the social context that are not subject to this kind of differentiation; I mean voluntary acts performed in the belief that they will benefit others and entailing neither obligation on the part of the volunteer nor any right or privilege on the part of the recipient.

As previously noted, when we think of the urge to contribute as an instinct, the correlation of rights to obligations is often the reverse of what it would seem, contrary to what our intuition tells us. Within this new way of thinking the sense of obligation diminishes and it becomes more natural to think in terms of rights.

Obligation towards Posterity: Maternal and Paternal Types

Most human instincts, whether physiological, such as hunger and sexual appetite, or psychological, like the urge to contribute, are common to both sexes, though perhaps in different degrees. The maternal instinct, however, is regarded as peculiarly female and is often seen as discrete from other instincts. Yet men also feel the special love that parents have for their children, so what kind of emotion is the love felt by a father for his children?

The uniquely female physiological instinct we call maternal love is in many cases limited to the relationship between a mother and her own children. In some mothers it has no substance outside that relationship, particularly in a social context. But because the love a mother feels for her children is so passionately devoted it is sometimes supplanted by harshness and decidedly unmotherly behaviour towards other children.

Although the same tendency exists in fathers, generally speaking they try to conceal it. Indeed, fathers have a tendency to be strict with their own children in order to train and discipline them. From its roots in what was in Japan a largely patriarchal social system, the tendency not to favour or spoil one's own children has been passed down as the traditional method of paternal childrearing and still characterizes the traditional Japanese father figure. In the typical father's case the physiological instinct towards his children undergoes a qualitative change, gradually becoming something like a sense of mission, which in turn leads to an effort to awaken his children to their own innate spirit of contribution.

Why are such gender-based differences evident in emotions such as the urge to contribute and parental love? Could it be that, in their respective attitudes to their children, women instinctively tend to try to fulfil their obligation towards their own generation, while the dominant tendency in men is towards fulfilling their social obligation to their posterity? Or perhaps we can say that a woman's instinct for fulfilling her obligation to posterity is governed primarily by the physiological factor of maternal love, while a man's idea of fulfilling the same obligation through his children is something like a sense of mission.

One could speculate that the typical male sense of obligation to posterity differs so markedly from the typical female as to suggest that the human male, being potentially able to father large numbers of children, has an innate capacity, in both thought and action, for coping with that potential. This is not a question of the superiority of either gender; in my view the mother and father should complement one another, working as one in the interests of their common posterity. But here again there must be a natural flow, like water trickling from high ground to low, of maternal love in the mother and a paternal sense of mission in the father.

Hypocrisy: The Opposite Extreme

If there is one thing I can genuinely claim to despise it is hypocrisy. The hypocrite often lies, but that does not mean that all lying is wrong.

For example, someone who conceals a physical illness in order to go on performing his duties cannot properly be called a hypocrite. For him, his duties are a necessity, taking priority over his illness. In other words, he identifies himself with the ability to fulfill his responsibilities and to lose that ability would be tantamount to losing his very sense of self.

Such a person's sense of self can be regarded as embedded in his own personal integrity and the sense of responsibility with which he seeks to carry out his appointed duties. His reason gives priority to an image of himself as someone who always completes what is expected of him and ultimately he comes to identify his duties as part of his self. If he were unable to fulfil his duties he would lose his sense of self, his sense of his own existence depends on being able to fulfil them. Underlying such behaviour is a keen sense of responsibility as well as an almost instinctive desire to avoid causing trouble for other people.

The hypocrite, in contrast, presents the despicable behaviour of someone who, under the guise of good intentions, exploits for his own gain the circumstances of people who need help. Most instances of hypocrisy – feigned virtue – take that form. In his value system the hypocrite has little or no recognition of others as people. Part of his conscious deception is to lie with the objective of appearing virtuous.

As we saw in Chapter 1, Plato posits 'the Good' as the single, supreme Idea or Form underlying all others and argues that the Good and Truth are ultimately the same thing. Hypocrisy, the pretence of goodness and truth, is immoral; to act hypocritically is to mock the truth and to disdain the essence of human nature.

Conflict

— based on a depiction of Achilles and Penthesilea on an Archaic-
period amphora. He who acts solely for his own sake is liable to
forsake even his human dignity. I seek a direction for society in the
type of person who actively rebukes that self-centred attitude, in the
paradigm of humanity I call *Homo contribuens*.

The hypocrite does not even attempt to discern the truth, but brazenly defies it, until he finally deceives even himself. This results in renouncing his pride as a human being and wantonly disregarding not only his own dignity but also the dignity of other people.

The hypocrite is guilty of inexcusable behaviour of the basest kind and the reason he is so heavily stigmatized as vile is that he dares to dismiss virtue in his heart while calmly pretending to be virtuous himself. Sometimes children who are too young to know right from wrong tell defensive or self-serving lies; that is not hypocrisy. A true hypocrite has to be intelligent, wily and knowledgeable. That is why, of course, it has become simple common sense not to judge people by their appearance or intelligence alone.

Hypocrisy is as rooted in the inclination to lie as the urge to contribute is rooted in instinct. The important thing is not that a person is able to act hypocritically towards others, but that he can do so towards himself as well. It is this ability to pretend virtue even in his own eyes that enables the hypocrite to brazenly deny what is good and right and disregard the essential truths of being human.

Moreover, because the hypocrite is wholly conscious of the fact that his feigned spirit of altruism is a fabrication based on lies, he knows in advance that his behaviour cannot ever be anything but bogus and nihilistic, unable to respond to what is essential to human nature.

I regard nihilism as the ultimate in selfishness. Some people succumb to nihilism when they are faced with their own death and that is because they lack the spiritual strength to accept objectively the inevitable end for every individual life. The kind of spiritual strength I mean is the profound and supple strength that Japanese call *mono no aware* (see Chapter 2). Nihilism encourages one to feel rejected by others, which makes a person retreat into a world entirely her or his own. Nihilists are often described as misanthropic, world-weary, pessimistic, even contemplative, but at heart the nihilist is self-centred and tormented by her/his own insatiable vanity and competitiveness. People caught in the vortex of such emotions gradually lose themselves in behaviour that serves no one's interests but their own. Perhaps that is their only channel to self-justification.

In that solipsistic world where 'others' have no real part to play, the nihilist actively squanders all opportunity to manifest the instinctive urge to contribute. This can lead to the abandonment of all dignity as a human being and subsequent total submersion into hypocrisy.

I will probably never fully know the true motives behind Takeshi's decision to reject nihilism and devote himself to study as he waited for death to take him. I believe, however, that he garnered the determination to do so through an encounter with a philosophical way of thinking that he recognized as being in tune with the very essence of human nature. If there is a way to save people from nihilism I suspect it lies in a philosophical awakening to instincts such as the urge to contribute and to ideas such as the sense of mission.

Ethics and Economics: Right and Wrong versus Profit and Loss

People judge right and wrong by ethical guidelines and calculate profit and loss by economic paradigms. In the world of social relationships we tend to bring a sense of duty or obligation to matters of right and wrong and a sense of rights to matters of profit and loss. People generally are more interested in their rights than their obligations, and today's world gives higher priority to economics than to ethics.

Children in many societies today have diminishing opportunities to develop a healthy sense of ethics. Parents and school teachers try to instil in children that this or that behaviour is 'wrong', but realistically, in these times it might be more effective

Scales

– based on a drawing by Leonardo da Vinci in *Reonarudo da Vinchi sobyoshu* [Drawings by Leonardo da Vinci] (published by Iwanami Shoten, 1985). The scales of right and wrong sometimes move by a calculation of profit and loss that is beyond ethics. To this mechanism, too, I want to be keenly attuned.

to teach children that unacceptable behaviour will incur some kind of 'loss'. Perhaps children understand 'loss' better than 'wrong', which only emphasizes how very difficult it is to foster moral sensibilities in the young.

In contrast, the calculation of profit and loss is relatively easy to teach. It could be worthwhile to cultivate children's ethical sensibilities by using examples relating to profit and loss when educating them about the different values involved in judging right from wrong and in calculating profit and loss, as well as about the relationship between the two. It would be ill-advised to teach children about calculating profit and loss without the corollary of them learning about right and wrong.

The rising incidence of juvenile crime, the decline of social morals and other signs of malaise can be attributed in part to a social climate in which decent people who do the right thing often are perceived to become disadvantaged, while wrongdoers reap great benefits. If this is true, then presumably such problems would be significantly reduced if we could transform our society into one where the virtuous profited and the wicked were punished. Whatever prevails, it is crucial that educational institutions instil in children a firm sense of ethics (right and wrong) as well as a sound sense of economics (profit and loss).

By doing what I consider to be morally right even when it appears to be to my disadvantage, I seek to enrich my life and work, to reaffirm my reason for living and to augment my edifying life-experience. What assures me that such behaviour ultimately serves my own interests is my conviction that the urge to contribute is an instinct. Someone who thinks this way with confidence can live a rewarding life that is in symmetry with all his or her life modes and free from domination by either his ethical sensibilities or the computation of profit and loss.

In the conventional view, good conduct is a virtue; I regard good conduct as a form of profit. This does not mean that someone who understands the urge to contribute as an instinct enjoys profit but lacks moral virtue; serving others' interests leads naturally to moral virtue.

Episode 4
The Hot-tempered King

Through his business my father, Fujitaro Taki, helped build the infrastructure of Japan's world-class urban rail systems. He had a fiery, Zeus-like personality; he expected his commands to be followed with absolute obedience and tended to react irrationally when angered. But he also had a more human, sometimes unpredictable side. I remember an anecdote from many years ago. . . . .

It was some time around 1956. My father's company had been notified by the tax office that it was late in filing its revised local tax return, which the entire accounting department was now hastening to complete. Upon learning that the company had incurred a surcharge of well over 100,000 yen for being late my father was furious. Having resolved not to use company funds to pay the surcharge he called in the employee responsible for the tax return and told him bluntly, 'This is your responsibility. You pay it'.

The amount of money involved was not large enough to have had any significant impact on the business and although the employee involved was certainly at fault for not ensuring the return was submitted on time, this punishment seemed to be nothing more than a spiteful way for my father to exact retribution.

Flatly refusing to listen to any argument my father even told the employee, 'If you don't pay the surcharge I'll make one of your relatives pay'. The employee went to the tax office and explained that because the late return was his fault the company would not pay the surcharge and he had to pay it himself. He could not afford to pay it all at once and so the tax office agreed to let him pay it off out of his own pocket in ten instalments.

As soon as the employee had made the tenth and final payment my father promptly reimbursed him in full. 'I was testing your good faith', he told him with a smile. It was quite obvious that the company should pay the surcharge but this is hardly the kind of remark most people would have made in the denouement to such an incident.

My father revealed his peculiar personality in various other ways as well. During Japan's traditional gift-giving seasons he was so concerned to prevent the department stores delivering the company's gifts directly to his clients that he would have them wrapped and addressed by his own staff – and only by employees who had served the company for many years as they were the only people he trusted.

Then there was his attitude to automated office equipment. In his view, desktop calculators, which at that time were just coming into general use, were no substitute for the manual tally; he made his accountants check their calculations in blue pencil every five lines, after which he himself would double check them in red pencil. The photocopier was another machine he distrusted because he did not understand how it worked. Ridiculous though it sounds, he would verify in red pencil every copy's fidelity to its original.

In Greek mythology, Zeus was furious when Prometheus took it upon himself to teach humans, whom Prometheus had created, how to use fire. Zeus was angry because he regarded fire as the root of evil. To punish Prometheus, Zeus bound him with bronze chains to a rocky mountainside and set an eagle to pick at his flesh day after day.

The gods of mythology – including the deities in the ancient Japanese myths recorded in the *Kojiki* (Record of Ancient Matters) – could be brutal, but they also had a familiar, thoroughly human side. I remember a day when my father was in the office corridor venting his rage at me with particular fury. Finally, I confronted him for being so hot-tempered and unreasonable, fully expecting this to be the last thing I ever said to him. For some reason he passed over to me the documents he had been holding and, pivoting on his walking stick, turned away. His face angled slightly back towards me, the rage now evident only in the set of his mouth, my father walked off, the scent of camphor from his suit lingering in his wake.

CHAPTER 5

PLAN FOR A NEW ERA
OF HUMANITY

ca

Embrace the changes that result as society progresses, fulfil your ascribed role, and a broad vision of the future will emerge.

Contributing and the Corporate Interest

How does the urge to contribute fit into today's corporate world? How do enterprise and business management function in terms of the urge to contribute? To begin with, the desire to protect and nurture the company one works for is comparable to the desire to protect and nurture one's own community. I say 'one's' community and company, but we are talking about collective entities and we should probably use the plural – *our* community, *our* company. However it is expressed, implicit in such references to an individual's relation to a company is the idea of an 'essence' of the company with which the individual identifies. This is an important consideration in business management and provides a good introduction for considering the nature of corporate society.

The way in which company employees speak of 'my company' conveys an attitude founded in more than their own individual concerns. There is a strong sense of their desire to protect and maintain the company and an understanding of the company as an arena in which they accord secondary status to their own personal interests in the interests of others. The term also implies the confederacy of a company that links one person with numerous other employees as colleagues. At work here is a perception in which the singular sense of 'my' is superseded by an attitude of mutual concern – a sense that 'my' interests and the interests of others are indivisible. Given each employee's identification with the group as 'my company', the resulting collective sense of belonging takes concrete form as a distinct corporate identity.

Business enterprises are fundamentally different from local, regional, or national communities in that businesses are profit-oriented organizations. Companies pay salaries and wages to their employees and taxes to their local and national governments. The relationship between business enterprises and their employees is in essence an economic contract. The contractual role of employees is to perform their appointed duties, their jobs. Their actions on the job are not voluntary or altruistic. Recalling the discussion of life modes in Chapter 2, the company can be thought of as an arena for action of a type belonging to a life mode different from that in which altruism operates.

A business enterprise is more than just its employees; perhaps even more important are its customers. A company sustains itself by receiving money from customers in exchange for the goods or services they request. Often business activities involve investors, stockholders, partners and subcontractors, who collectively comprise the corporate sector as a whole. All of these relationships are based on a form of economic contract.

Essentially, business enterprises are profit-seeking organizations whose sphere of activity is the free market. In accordance with free-market principles, dumping, monopolies and other practices that create unfair advantages for specific companies are prohibited by law and the fair trade commission acts as a watchdog to prevent such opportunism. These conditions virtually guarantee fierce competition. On initial examination, then, it may appear that in the business community it makes little sense to proceed in the mode of contribution for the benefit of others. The corporate world would appear to be essentially an arena for vigorous activity in the mode of work.

Because the rules of business vary from one country or society to another, it is difficult to encompass all business in universal terms, like the axioms of immutable truth and essential human reality that we discussed in Chapter 1. Corporate rules and practices vary widely by location and also in time. Consider, for example, the practice of rewarding customers with gifts or bonuses; in Japan it is legal for credit card companies to present gifts to current cardholders who introduce new customers, while in Germany this practice is considered illegal.

On the other hand, some market principles are constant and universal. They relate to aspects of the business world that are not subject to laws or government guidelines, which, without exception, vary according to time and place. These constant elements may provide a basis for determining an underlying 'corporate philosophy' ['rationale of business'], which, if it were identified, might reveal the essence of corporation [the essential reality of business], just as sufficient probing and analysis evidence an essential reality of human existence.

In Chapter 13, Book 4 of his *Principles of Economics*, British economist Alfred Marshall highlights the importance of credit (goodwill, trust) in business, noting that 'success brings credit and credit brings success; credit and success help to retain old customers and to bring new ones'. This expresses an understanding of goodwill as an absolute yardstick and essential element of the corporate ideal. Inherent in that way of thinking is a desire to generate value for both the business community and society in general. This supports the notion of 'socially-oriented' business that neither contributes through welfare-type social activities nor gears its activities solely towards the pursuit of profit. Such a corporate philosophy [business rationale] can be reflected in and implemented through the entrepreneur's vision, but, as will be expounded later, corporate visions often get swept away by insistent pressures of change.

In my view, the circumstances that give rise to goodwill depend on the spirit of private enterprise in its adherence to the fundamental principles underlying the flux of variable market conditions. Those circumstances must be a projection of the essential nature of private enterprise that does not change with the passing of time or from one country to the next. Business management operates within a context of strict adherence to those principles, and goodwill is created on that basis. The philosophy [rationale] of a corporate society is thus essentially an adherence to law and is based on an understanding of that law as absolute. Insofar as we call this a 'philosophy', it must entail a form of 'essence', and insofar as it is a philosophy of private enterprise, it must entail a subjective will to serve society as well as the 'phenomena' that sustain corporate activities. Only from this vantage point can we begin to understand the urge to contribute in the context of corporate activities.

It is my observation that goodwill and trust are born of a conservatism in the spirit of corporate management that operates to uphold market principles no matter how actual market conditions change from place to place or over time. Such an enterprise endures despite changes and variations of time and place because it embraces the kind of business management that maintains an absolute commitment to uphold market principles under any circumstances. That is the premise that gives rise to goodwill and trust. The philosophy of corporate society is, in the final analysis, a commitment to adhere to the law and understanding that law as absolute. Any true philosophy has an essential core; at the core of the basic corporate philosophy is the imperative to positively contribute to society. That is the only genuine corporate rationale. Because of that imperative an enterprise must conduct itself in a manner that ensures its activities endure. If we look at business

97

and enterprise in this way, we finally make sense of how the urge to contribute fits into corporate activities.

The Social Role of Private Enterprise

Private enterprise plays an important role in supporting the life and economy of a society. It develops things that people need, producing them as commercial products, supplying them to the market at appropriate prices, and so on. That role has already expanded into many areas of society and will undoubtedly continue doing so into the future. The spread of the market economy has aided the development of transportation networks, fuelled employment, and created greater effective demand. Corporate research and development aimed at meeting the rising demand are also pivotal in our everyday lives. Drawing on the advances of science methods are devised to adapt ever more precise and complex technologies for the benefit of consumers. Commercial enterprise and society have, in a sense, created a relationship of mutual benefit: while business fosters growth in various parts of society, people in society support production by private enterprise.

Clearly, the continued vitality of private enterprise is crucial, not only for the corporate sector but also for society as a whole. When a company is described as a 'going concern' it promotes the image of a stable, developing and mutually beneficial relationship between producers and consumers, between private enterprise and the wider society. The evolving private sector is always eager to sustain the mutually profitable relationship with consumers and that eagerness manifests in tangible ways, such as products and finance, or in intangible ways like goodwill, trust and interdependence. Writing on the importance of the 'intangible property' that sustains growing enterprises, American economist John R. Commons asserts that goodwill and trust are the lifeblood of a going concern. (Cited in Shozo Kono, *Going Concerns no Keieigaku*

[Management Studies on Going Concerns], Tokyo: Zeimu Keiei Kyokai, 1996.) In other words, the future of any business enterprise depends on its contribution to society and on the goodwill and trust it maintains with the consumers who benefit from that contribution.

Even a company that can boast a high degree of customer satisfaction with its products may offend if something in its attitude is objectionable. Or even if a company has an attitude that pleases everyone it can still lose customers by failing to offer an overall product line that satisfies them. Together with creating jobs, which has a direct economic effect, supplying products and generating goodwill and trust are key components of the private sector's social role. Trust and goodwill arise in the corporate context only when profit-seeking endeavours are juxtaposed with other, less tangible goals. It is in this arena that the business sector needs to assert its own kind of urge to contribute.

Many societies today are sufficiently advanced and mature to demand that private enterprise not only plays its part in market competition but also explores the potential for more vigorous, new and ambitious applications of the urge to contribute. A company imbued with those goals will strive to meet its customers' evolving needs, serve its own interests and do its utmost to make the world around it a better place. 'Value-added' is generally understood to be a direct source of profit for a business enterprise, but the management approach I am proposing – based on careful maintenance of goodwill and trust in the relationship with one's customers – would generate for society a form of value added that is much more than the value of products. Call it an institutional urge to contribute, or some other name, but when a business enterprise as a whole adopts such an attitude, even though it may at first seem unrelated to profit, I believe that enterprise actually generates new forms of value-added.

New Owners of Private Enterprise

The complex fabric of interwoven systems in today's society makes huge demands on commercial enterprises and their employees just to keep pace with the constantly mobile business environment. Such conditions exert a great deal of pressure at both the organizational and employee levels, creating a situation that has important implications for the way we consider the nature of and prospects for contemporary society.

Today's complex environment requires a new approach to management that goes beyond the idea of employment as a one-dimensional, one-way relationship. There is a need to recreate the two-way dynamic achieved when a company strives to keep its employees satisfied and employees commit to achieving the company's objectives; the company must also maintain its profit-making function while continuing to fulfil its role in society. The foundation of all these activities should be the urge to contribute. In my own, very basic model for improved company management, the company acts on its urge to contribute in relation to its employees and the employees act on their urge to contribute in relation to the company; the outcome benefits both, a consequence of which is a significant benefit for society.

However, current conditions make this approach far from easy, particularly in Japan, where the repercussions from the wave of bankruptcy and personnel retrenchment that followed the early-1990s collapse of its asset-inflated economy are still being felt. But even under these conditions, the urge to contribute, to identify one's own concerns with those of others, can serve as the basis for a new paradigm of labour-management relations that offers a breakthrough to a bright new era for companies and employees alike. This model of industrial relations was once a distinguishing feature of Japanese-style management, and many would agree that the time has come for us to take another close look at that tradition.

The practice of truth
– based on a drawing by Leonardo da Vinci in *Reonarudo da Vinchi sobyoshu* [Drawings by Leonardo da Vinci] (published by Iwanami Shoten, 1985). The flesh is weak, and practicing the truth can be gruelling. But the armour of reason that philosophy provides is harder than the hardest metal, and is dependable in that struggle.

Meanwhile, a new and troubling problem for corporations has arisen involving the increasing impact of employee pension funds on management authority. This unprecedented situation is affecting corporate management at a basic level, is propelling the drive for corporate takeovers and personnel retrenchment and is sweeping the world with a force that could reorder the very fabric of society, including Japan's. Far from being a concern for management alone, it has serious consequences for employees and, by extension, society as a whole.

In the United States it is estimated that employee pension funds now exceed two-fifths of the value of all stocks of listed companies and more than two-thirds that of the top thousand listed companies. In the past, it was common practice for companies to launch new enterprises or expand their existing businesses using funds from investors, but in recent years this approach seems to be adopted only within limited contexts. In the prevailing climate, investment in private enterprise is coming increasingly from individuals, including employees, through the management of pension funds. Thus, effective ownership of private enterprise is transferring to individuals, including company employees, activating the emergence of a new business environment wherein the social role of the conventional investor is coming to an end; employees as a group are replacing them as the de facto owners of private enterprise and individual investors are becoming archetypal stockholders.

Because the business environment can be seen as a fluctuating continuum in the market economy, it suggests the potential for a new philosophy of private enterprise to actively take root in society based on this emerging principle.

I see the changes taking place in the business environment as an advance towards maximising the capabilities of the individual in society. In this new context, employees of commercial enterprises will reject outmoded business stereotypes and utilize their company's collective strengths to their own advantage.

Furthermore, by pooling their strengths and resources, employees as a collective can turn their own original ideas into 'their' company's profit. Acting on those ideas, more and more employees can achieve an even stronger sense of identification with their company and actively share in its corporate vision, a privilege that until now was exclusive to the corporate owners.

Conversely, this trend towards socialization of ownership can also be expected to promote innovations in management, production and marketing and, ultimately, to precipitate factors that could operate against the individual employee, including personnel cuts, open-shop employment and mergers and acquisitions. Hence, if employees lose their sense of the company as an arena for actualising individual capabilities their company spirit will die and the company will no longer provide the locus from where they can activate their urge to contribute.

In the September-October 1988 issue of *Harvard Business Review*, P. F. Drucker addressed this problem in connection with new ways of managing pension funds that promote corporate takeovers and threaten business management, describing such an approach as an outright attack on company employees. That a mere threat can kill the morale of management, even middle–management and specialists who effectively run the company, suggests a disdain for the steady, honest work of creating wealth and a flaunting of the primacy of the money game. While acknowledging the inevitability of an increasing emphasis on profit in pension management, Drucker warns against uncurbed exploitation of pension funds.

Neither managers nor employees can afford to be thrown off balance by these seemingly drastic changes in the business environment. In my view, the primary duty of everyone involved in an enterprise is to sustain the company. That is where they must direct their efforts, neither endorsing nor opposing the changes but adapting to them as the evolving reality of the market environment. This underlies the rationale for a constant, unvarying business philosophy that allows us to incorporate such change and accept it as inevitable. In the United States, as individuals begin to accept the inexorable trend towards pension fund finance a new corporate philosophy is in fact already emerging.

Japan's corporate sector has a long tradition of lifetime employment. On the strength of this tradition employment in Japan has nurtured the individual's basic needs, both in personal life and in his/her life in the community, to a degree rarely, if ever, practised anywhere else in the world. While some predict that the tradition of lifetime employment will soon be outmoded, I firmly believe that if it fits Japan's circumstances Japan should revive and refurbish the tradition rather than imitate the practices of other countries. I also believe that it is precisely when conditions are conducive to retrenchment and takeovers that we need to embrace an ethos that fosters company spirit. When the joint-stock company system was transmitted to Japan from the West in the late nineteenth century, the founders of modern Japanese business accepted the reality of resource-poor Japan's conditions and worked with them. Following this example, companies today should accept the current corporate climate and develop new and unique management methods best suited to that climate. To focus only on the negative effects of the prevailing business conditions on one's company is an introverted perspective that serves no useful purpose.

Pension fund investment is often short-lived and profit-driven and comes to an end once it exceeds market value on the stock market. While it may initially stimulate a range of economic innovations, in the context of Japan, where the company is traditionally regarded as a place of lifelong commitment and a mainstay of community stability, pension fund investment would be unsuitable and its unpredictability harmful.

Japan's business sector should take a more positive approach towards the socialization of ownership – a trend that is now also sweeping Japan – and draw on the existing tradition of lifetime employment as the template for future progress. If current changes in business practices cause employees to lose their sense of identification with 'their' company, Japanese companies may find difficulty even surviving. Just as Americans are comfortable with the open-shop employment system, in Japan the union-shop system is familiar and perfectly acceptable. There is good reason to suppose that by continuing to work within their own traditions, Japanese companies and their employees can withstand downsizing and other cataclysms in the business environment and eventually restore the level of prosperity Japanese business once enjoyed.

Donations and Taxation

No country can equal the United States in either the quality or quantity of its art collections, both classical and contemporary. As a former director of the Metropolitan Museum of Art once pointed out, American collections originally consisted of little more than Native American crafts and some Dutch-made works of silver and ceramics. How and why has a country with such humble artistic beginnings so clearly overtaken everyone in the wealth of its art collections?

The original endowment for America's first national art museum, the National Gallery of Art in Washington D.C., was bestowed by Andrew W. Mellon, whose art works formed the nucleus of its holdings. In 1937, Mellon donated his collection to the museum and provided funds for the building through the Mellon financial group. Mellon expressed his desire to establish a national art museum in a letter to President Franklin D. Roosevelt.

December 22, 1936

My dear Mr. President:
Such a gallery would be for the use and benefit of the general public; and it is my hope that it may attract gifts from other

citizens who may in the future desire to contribute works of art of the highest quality to form a great national collection. In connection, therefore, with the intended gift, I shall stipulate that the proposed building shall not bear my name, but shall be known as 'The National Art Gallery' or by such other name as may appropriately identify it as a gallery of art of the national Government.

A letter of A. W. Mellon to Franklin D. Roosevelt

December 22nd, 1936

(The American Presidency Project [online])

Reports of this munificent gift from Mellon to his country reverberated among America's wealthy elite. Subsequently, beginning while the National Gallery building was still under construction, letter after letter arrived from prominent private art collectors offering to donate to the museum many of the world's finest works of painting, sculpture and craft.

A range of factors prompted this chorus of potential donors. First, aspiring donors sympathized with Mellon's intentions. He had donated his own collection and endowed the building, but rather than naming it after himself he chose to collaborate with the government and named it instead the National Gallery of Art. This allowed others with art works gathering dust in their stately homes to donate them in a manner that satisfied their sense of patriotism. The National Gallery provided a forum to make those works available not as objects of speculation or investment but as cultural assets accessible to everyone.

Another factor was the donor-friendly American tax system, which provided incentives for the redistribution of wealth by making public-spirited donations and contributions tax-deductible for individuals and organizations. Furthermore, to encourage donations of art by foundations and other sources, the tax system allowed the amount of each deduction to be based on the current market value of the piece of art. In other words, if an artwork purchased years earlier for $10,000 but with a market value in the current tax year of $100,000 were donated to a museum, the amount deductible from the donor's taxable income would be calculated on the basis of $100,000, not $10,000. American income tax laws have since been revised and the deductible amount is now based on the original purchase price, not the current market value. Even so, in the United States and other developed countries such donations still do not incur the enormous donation and gift taxes that they do in Japan.

It is worth reflecting on what Mellon wrote to Roosevelt: expressing the wishes of a businessman who had been one of America's leading bankers and later secretary of the treasury, Mellon wanted to give some of his wealth back to the society that had enabled him to build his fortune. Business is purposeless without society. The desire to give back to the people the wealth generated by business is natural, thus such donations and contributions are inspired by that desire. In comparison, Japan's peculiar tax system, by which such philanthropic acts incur prohibitive taxes, seems wholly unreasonable and should be revised.

NPOs and the Social Contribution of Private Enterprise

Since private enterprise is one of the most vital forces in society we can expect the urge to contribute to grow into a new dynamic in the business world. In fact, over the past few years an increasing number of organizations have been making social contributions that go beyond the traditional scope of business activities.

Peter Drucker predicted that nonprofit organizations – NPOs – would be a key growth sector in the twenty-first century. If Drucker is right, the NPO sector will continue to expand, partly for reasons related to the socialization of ownership in private enterprise described earlier in this chapter. In a business environment buffeted by restructuring, downsizing and takeovers, company spirit sinks to a low ebb; employees and others lose the sense of being part of a larger entity to which they are making a contribution. As they seek other ways to satisfy the urge to contribute they reject the company framework in favour of volunteer activities.

Evidence of such a development is particularly striking in the proliferation of non-governmental organizations (NGOs). Despite their growth, however, when considered in comparison with the way profit-seeking enterprises contribute to society, NGOs and NPOs generate some large, practical issues.

NPO and NGO activities have traditionally been focused on medicine, social welfare, environmental protection, disaster relief, human rights and education, but more recently they have begun to expand into culture, the arts, sports, community improvement, international cooperation, peace activities, minority and women's issues and others. The common distinguishing feature of these organizations is that they are private and non-profit-oriented, whether legally incorporated or not, their activities are similar and have the same rationale. The term non-profit organization evolved out of the American corporate and tax systems and the stress on non-profit-seeking is deliberate. 'Non-governmental organization' developed out of the constellation of activities linked to the United Nations and emphasizes the international character of the activity for which the NGO was organized to carry out. As the term implies, they operate independently of any specific government.

In Japan, people tend to use 'NPO' for organizations focused on local activities within the country and 'NGO' for agencies involved in international cooperation overseas. In fact, the boundaries are not so clearly drawn; there are environmentalist NGOs, for example, involved in local environmental projects with national or local government assistance, and there are NPOs involved in international programmes, like medicine and public health. Since both types of organization focus on social welfare projects their activities are bound to be virtually the same, but largely because of their different origins – indicated by the different designations, NPO versus NGO – they have promoted competition, futile debates and power struggles between the 'American school' and the 'UN school'.

Whether NPO or NGO, the corporate or tax systems affecting a non-profit activity and the nature of the organization that initiated the activity are not directly relevant to the nature of the activity itself. However, when it comes to implementing a project, you cannot ignore the type of organization, the tax system under which it operates and the arrangements of incorporation on which its finances rest.

What is problematic in both designations is the 'non' prefix. It declares what these organizations are *not* – not for profit, not associated with any government – but it says little about what they *are*. Neither NPO nor NGO as a category excludes non-profit and non-governmental activities that are also antisocial, subversive, or worse. In my opinion, what should be emphasized in any such organization whose motives are genuine is the desire to contribute through their activities rather than their non-profit or non-governmental credentials. They should be acknowledged in terms of their first priority: making a contribution to the common good without regard to profit for any specific organization or the interests of any specific nation.

To the extent that this idea is gaining credibility and wider application, Peter Drucker's prediction is being realised. 'Contribution-oriented organizations', which during the twentieth century emerged in the gap between profit-seeking organizations (corporations, industries) and public organizations (local governments, national governments, the United Nations), seem destined to become an important third type of organization in this century and a major force in the totality of social welfare activity.

The profit-seeking corporate sector will probably feel increasing pressure to restructure its relations in order to interact not only with governmental bodies but also with the emerging 'third sector' of non-profit organizations. One effect will be to redirect corporate efforts away from 'non-contributive' profit-seeking activities towards a new paradigm of corporate behaviour whereby profit is generated by contributing to the common good. The current upsurge in corporate social contributions and active discourse about corporate social responsibility may indeed be precursors of this reconfiguration of the business environment.

The same shift can be seen in the One Per cent Club, which was launched by the Keidanren (Japan Federation of Economic Organizations) in 1990. It is an attempt to institute arrangements under which companies contribute one per cent of their ordinary profits and individuals one per cent of their disposable income to social welfare activities. Still fresh in the memory of many people is the prominent role played by a group of One Per cent Club members in NPO-led relief activities following the Kobe earth-quake of 1995.

Among other signs of change in thinking is the matching gift system, which commits companies to contribute to organizations that carry out volunteer activities. An increasing number of companies are encouraging pro bono work by their employees through paid 'volunteer leave' and other company schemes. Company-NPO collaboration is another form of contribution emerging in recent years, enabling NPOs to participate in corpo-rate social welfare activities, select the beneficiaries of corporate assistance, or even participate in a company's main business, perhaps by helping it to develop new products that benefit both the NPO and the company.

Insofar as these activities are in accord with the conventional objectives of private enterprise while at the same time incorpo-rating social contribution, we can expect them to increasingly characterize corporate behaviour in the twenty-first century. For one thing, they represent an improvement in some of the ways contributions have been handled. When the corporate sector carries out contributive activities in a dimension entirely separate from regular profit-seeking operations, it is too easy for those activities to become constrained by doctrinal or even dogmatic aims, rather than practical ends directed towards improving someone's situation. Also, if there is a downturn in business performance, unprofitable social contributions are likely to be curtailed.

By altering our perspective we can create a new paradigm of corporate activity that combines the mode of work (profit-seeking activities) with the mode of contribution (socially beneficial activities). In this new vision, corporate behaviour can operate with a more resolute human approach than is possible in a single-track mode and it opens up new prospects for private enterprise in the twenty-first century.

Environmental Efforts

The natural environment is on the threshold of global crisis, making it imperative for environmental issues to be addressed both regionally and internationally. Human beings are implicated in all of the worst environmental problems we face today and those problems are immense, exacerbated by the accumulation of all environmental damage generated by individuals, communities, or companies. Underlying the critical situation facing us is the anthropocentric hubris that has blinded humanity to its responsibility to preserve and nurture the natural world that sustains us. The predicament of the environment is today recognized with more clarity than ever before and efforts to repair the global ecosystem have rapidly gained momentum in recent years.

The impetus for major environmental efforts today is on reversing the destruction wrought from the myopic, self-serving exploitation by humans and restoring and nurturing the natural world. We might look at the environmental movement as an expression by humanity as a whole, of the collective urge to contribute, played out with a global perspective by people acting on behalf of the health of our planet, which becomes an 'other' whose interests we wish to serve. Yet some aspects of today's environmentalism do not represent a genuinely altruistic spirit of contributing. Let me elaborate by examining some environmental issues in terms of the urge to contribute.

One is the need to conserve fossil fuels such as oil and coal. These are limited resources and their conservation is vital to the long-term health of the economy, while at the same time they are dangerously polluting. Nuclear power offers one alternative energy source but is viewed with anxiety because of the dangers it poses to human health and to the environment. Another issue is chloro-fluorocarbons, which are now banned because of their destructive effect on the ozone layer. Many familiar and newly developed substances, in practice, generating severe greenhouse-gas effects that are causing new levels of public concern.

The list of environmental problems goes on: overuse of fertilizers, pesticides and herbicides in agriculture has led to pollution of land and water, and, together with devastating floods, cutting, planting and development policies caused the desertification of vast tracts of land. Combined with difficulties in producing and distributing enough food where it is needed, the damage caused by shortsighted agricultural practices has created overwhelming problems. One of the most serious is the challenge of feeding people in regions experiencing steady and high population growth, as in parts of Africa and South East Asia. For decades, the United States, the world's largest food exporter, has continued to develop unrestricted large-scale agribusiness, justifying its policy as a way to 'help alleviate the food crisis', but the methods used deplete underground water reserves, accelerate soil degradation, drive small farmers off their land, run rivers dry and leave toxic residues in soil and water. The ecological disruption of vast prairie lands in the central United States is a case in point. According to reports, these lands have been so irreparably damaged by the methods of mega-scale agribusiness that even if the region were left fallow, it would take many years for the soil to recover and an estimated tens of thousands of years just to replenish the underground water reserves.

That exemplifies just one more lamentable scenario in the story of humankind, set in motion when people use nature indiscriminately for human ends and ultimately destroy the very resources they depended on in the beginning. The irony is that even our responses to such problems have been totally self-centred. Some behaviour that seemed necessary to society results in damage to the environment that irritates, troubles and inconveniences people, who respond by promoting solutions that are more 'egological' than ecological.

It is nevertheless incumbent upon society to maintain surveillance over the environment and restore its balance even if the reasons for so doing are ultimately selfish. But when good intentions are too narrowly concentrated on a specific part of nature, they can lapse into self-serving practices that only lead to further destruction of nature. We have to be vigilant to combat this tendency, beginning with a radical rethinking of the basic ideas behind many of the environmental activities being carried out today.

Even declarations on the global environment made at G8 meetings, the Earth Summit, and other international conferences evidence an entirely anthropocentric attitude to these problems. Such an approach will never work, in my estimation, because it retains the basic premise of human priority that led the human race down the route of reckless development in the first place. For humans it is a stalemate and for the planet a growing disaster.

Humans, all humans, have to rethink their exclusively self-interested assumptions. We need to rekindle the collective instinct to contribute to the natural environment as an 'other' in need. If we can do this, our environmental efforts will take on a more effectively global character.

Meanwhile, besides untrammelled development, there is another major factor exacerbating the depletion of fossil fuel resources, erosion of the ozone layer, environmentally damaging agricultural practices and a raft of other problems and that is overpopulation. Continuing population growth directly affects the plight of the global environment; from food supply, natural resources and energy, to production and consumption, it impacts on virtually everything that is critical to sustaining both human life and the life of other creatures.

The only effective way to address the environmental problems that have emerged from overpopulation, overdevelopment and other factors is to tackle them from a broad, international perspective. This will entail compromises, sacrifices and above all, a new way of thinking. Inevitably, conditions of everyday life for individuals and communities are elements in the motives for environmental protection, and environmental preservation actions in any given region can have serious implications for the lives of the people who live there. Campaigns against companies that exploit a region's natural resources, for example, can have negative economic effects causing reduced employment and diminishing local revenues in those regions. On the other hand, how we respond to the forces that threaten the world's environment will affect the fate of all Earth's creatures, including humans. One campaign that deserves optimum support, therefore, is a campaign to encourage people all over the world to change their thinking and, guided by their urge to contribute, judge it their *right* to take these issues in hand and find solutions that will assure the long-term stability of our Earth and all its natural abundance.

The Urge to Contribute and the Sanctity of Life

The depletion of resources by overpopulation and irresponsible development has been happening while regional disparities in national income, means of production, and so on continue to widen. The prevalence of such remarkable differentials is the dark side of the capitalist economic system. There is a school of thought that considers the current capitalist system to have already become dysfunctional, assuming the impossibility of effective countermeasures.

At the same time, I have the impression that many people who live under one or another type of capitalism are beginning to take cognisance of the nagging voice of their instinctive urge to contribute, but are frustrated. They cannot find ways to satisfy that urge; their frustration needs an outlet, coming as it does out of an instinctual drive and I believe this quest for fulfilment is behind the rising wave of NPO and NGO activity.

The history of human society, of people working together in community, goes back further than records have been kept, but from evidence at least five thousand years old we know that human beings have witnessed calamity and adversity over many millennia. Again and again they have seen crime, war and genocide. Yet even so, in a broad sense, human societies have continued to devise modes of production and have learned to value human life as sacred and inviolable. I am convinced that the urge to contribute has played a determining role in this brighter side of our development, operating from deep within as a basic instinct. Many crises have arisen which could have fatally interrupted our cycle of life had this instinct not existed. It may be, in fact, that the continuance of our species is attributable to our instinctive urge to contribute.

Well-intentioned actions by specific groups, including corporate social welfare projects and community volunteer activities, can often seem self-serving to those outside the groups. From a certain perspective, the not-in-my-back yard attitudes mentioned in Chapter 3, for example, present an image of elementary self-interest. But if we regard the urge to contribute as human instinct, we can reasonably predict that these apparent contradictions will eventually be resolved and the dignity of humanity preserved. This is because human beings have an instinctive desire to help others in need. The action they take to help resolve others' problems arises not from a sense of obligation but rather from a predetermined desire and a sense that they have the *right* so to do.

If humanity as a whole could intellectualise this sense of right, the urge to contribute would become a force empowering humans to realize the nobility of which they are capable. As for individuals, each of us would express the urge to contribute by seeking to improve others' lives *for our own sake* and in so doing the happiness and well-being of humanity as a whole would increase immeasurably.

Imagine the six billion-plus people living on this planet working together to improve each other's lives and sustain the cycle of life for future generations. The effect would be transforming, a powerful testimony to the instinctive nature of the urge to contribute.

My Country, Other Countries

Sometimes political or social policies operate to constrain our instinctive responses, and because the constraints vary across cultures and nations, it can be difficult to identify the same urge to contribute as an instinct common to all people of whatever country or culture. If the urge to contribute really is an instinct, however, it is reasonable to think that any political regime whose policies subjugate that urge will, because it runs counter to nature, eventually crumble. Let us consider how the urge to contribute is manifested at the level of the nation.

Human community can be visualized in geographical units beginning with villages and towns and widening to cities, counties, states, nations and finally to the international community as a whole. A nation covers a substantial geographical area and generally comprises some level of diversity in its population.

When society is evolving in new directions, in very broad terms, some people adapt to and embrace change as decision-makers while some follow the decisions made by others. The

Opinion leader astride a horse

– based on a depiction of Hephaestus on an Archaic-period water bottle. Society cannot afford to ignore opinion leaders who pioneer innovations and pass them on to others. While most people walk, opinion leaders ride on the backs of horses, constantly advancing ahead of the crowd.

former are opinion leaders and the latter attend to the leaders' opinions before formulating or expressing their own. Whether a particular viewpoint is acceptable to the wider populace is often circumscribed by the stance of the opinion leaders.

In marketing, for example, opinion leaders are monitored for the purpose of formulating quantitative models for market forecasts. It is necessary to provide those opinion leaders with information about a certain product, how it compares with and differs from similar products, for example, in a fair and impartial evaluation. The disclosure of information to opinion leaders is important in other areas of social life also; if the merit of any social innovation is to be fairly assessed, full and unbiased information must be made available. The same can be said for society as a whole. Information disclosure is an indispensable part of the process by which knowledge established by opinion leaders is disseminated among opinion followers. In that way, the common store of knowledge and opinion in a society is formed through the interaction of its individual members.

Perhaps this provides a clue for resolving problems stemming from the pursuit of self-interests restricted solely to the immediate locality. By the formulation of just and fair views through proper information disclosure and the transmission and dissemination of those views to the general populace/opinion followers, local conflicts of interest could be resolved within the larger framework of the society as a whole. How the urge to contribute is manifested at the local community level is also closely related to the resolution of conflicts of interest between one community and another. It is another arena where opinion leaders and information dissemination play a decisive role.

Local and national governments are independent activists with the authority to make and implement decisions under their respective jurisdictions. At the same time, popular sovereignty requires the people to be vigilant and ensure that their government does not act against the interests of the populace. The people are obliged to demand rectification of improper or faulty procedures, including inadequate disclosure of information. In this relationship between the state and the people, the people must also monitor the government to prevent bias arising towards certain localities in the practical application by the government of the urge to contribute.

In Europe and the United States, there are people who act as ombudsmen to monitor the government on behalf of the citizenry. Japan does not have such a system in the public sector, but it does have autonomous volunteer and citizens' groups that monitor the behaviour of local governments. Known as 'citizen ombudsmen', these groups request disclosure of specific information about government spending and act as watchdogs guarding against improper entertainment activities, false statements of business trips, and any other misuse of public money by government officials. Seventy-two of these 'city ombudsmen' groups attended a national conference of watchdog organizations that was held in 1998.

A government is an institution, a corporate body, composed of persons usually elected by the people it serves, not a singular entity; but if a government is functioning properly by clearly reflecting the will of the people, then it must also reflect the collective urge to contribute of the individuals that comprise that society. Such collective expression of the urge to contribute implicitly differs from an individual's contributive instinct simply because it is the sum total, or the largest common denominator, of the contributive urges of many individuals. But the representative will can also be regarded as precisely this kind of common denominator and in that sense the collective urge to contribute can be considered the aggregate of the total animus.

Furthermore, we can consider the urge to contribute of an entire nation as a totality in relation to the corresponding totality of every other nation; that is, each nation's urge to contribute reflects the collective will of its own people. If a nation concentrates on its own interests and does not fulfil its role in the global community, its urge to contribute can degenerate into selfishness. Thus, if it hopes to fulfil its role in the international community it must never allow the will to serve others – an instinctive desire of each of its citizens – to transmute into national self-interests.

The first half of the twentieth century was an age of national egos in confrontation, culminating in two world wars of unprecedented magnitude. My purpose here, however, is not to retrace that tragic past but rather to propose a vision for the future.

The idea that the urge to contribute is an instinct offers a basis for preventing such national self-seeking from surfacing again. When a nation becomes completely absorbed in its own national interests, its people's urge to contribute may find natural expression within the country, but towards other countries that nation will exhibit only selfishness. On the understanding that the urge to contribute vis-à-vis other countries is a fundamental prerequisite for their own survival, nations must manifest that urge by identifying their own interests with those of other nations. This idea of a collective, national urge to contribute to other nations as part of one's own 'national instinct' is, I believe, the key to a better world in the twenty-first century. If this way of thinking permeated the people of every country at the individual level, then mutual consideration and cooperation – identifying 'our' interests with 'their' interests – would become the norm even at the level of international relations.

Recent years have been difficult and for many, unhappy. Not only Japan, but many parts of the world have experienced political troubles, economic dysfunction, deterioration of educational standards, accidents at nuclear power plants and a general degradation of public morals and standards. In addition, earthquakes, volcanic eruptions and other major natural disasters have disrupted many regions in the last few decades. Some countries have had to endure even greater burdens, long wars, continuing violence, disease, and hunger.

People are discouraged, but they do not succumb. Activities originating in the desire to help others and contribute to the common good keep appearing in every corner of society. It is important that these fledgling efforts be nurtured so that they can grow and spread. When disasters like the Kobe earthquake occur, rescue teams come from all over the world to help. The world is full of people ready and willing to extend a helping hand to others in adversity, even when they are on the other side of the planet. We must not overlook the power of this positive side of humanity, a light that continues to burn amid the darkness of our trouble-stricken world.

In the global perspective, the glow of one individual's urge to contribute may seem small and faint, but as an increasing number of people come together to pool the energy generated by that urge, the light will shine ever more brightly. I fervently hope that Japan, like other nations, will continue to feed and spread this light throughout the world. I do what I can as an individual to keep my own small flame as strong and bright as possible and trust that many others will do the same.

Episode 5
A Chinese Mau Suit

The city of Tianjin on China's east coast was enveloped by a cold weather system that had moved across from the continental interior. At dusk a light snow began to flutter down. Walking through the high-rise quarter, where a hush was quickly descending along with the twilight, my wife and I turned toward a still-bustling market area flooded with gaudy neon lights. At the fish market a woman, a lady of some refinement judging by her clothes, was at a stall buying a small portion of cod with scrupulous care.

Before long the snow turned into cold sleet. We started looking around for a restaurant in which to take shelter. Glancing down a side street off the main thoroughfare, I noticed a small old man in a traditional Chinese-style tunic suit gazing up at the stormy sky with his hands pressed together as if in prayer. My wife had not seen him; she was busy looking around for a restaurant. We hurried under the eaves of a nearby food store to shelter from the rain and because I wanted to take a longer look at the incongru-ous old man.

The store attendant approached us with a smile, but my attention was riveted on the old man looking up into the cold rain, hands pressed together. Without even knowing what they were I bought a few items of food that the storekeeper offered us. As I took the parcel I pointed out the old man to my wife.

'Maybe it's some kind of old kung-fu practice', she wondered out loud. The man's behaviour did look like something of that kind. Then again, perhaps he had simply lost his mind.

Holding his joined hands close to his puny chest, every now and then he uttered a few words. Although we were too far away to hear his voice, he appeared to be reciting something. The tunic suit he was wearing started to change colour as it got wet, but the old man seemed as oblivious to the rain as he was to the stares of the people around him.

'Yes', I concurred with my wife, 'probably a ritual of some ancient martial art or other'. The peculiar tension around the man did have the aura of a traditional martial discipline. His scarecrow-thin figure seemed utterly detached from us all, indifferent to the hubbub of the surrounding market.

Glancing behind me into the store, I noticed that the attendant and some customers were eyeing the old man with faint, disdainful smiles. Chinese drum and flute music was coming out of a CD player on an old lacquered cupboard with an arabesque design in gold and silver.

The ice-cold rain was falling harder now, enveloping the old man in a thin halo of water vapour as it bounced off his clothes. The deep indigo of his tunic suit glowed through the misty outline.

Gazing at the bluish luminescence of this tiny old man's rain-spattered clothes, I said, almost in a whisper, 'It's a prayer'. It seemed as if a prayer was visibly radiating from his frail old body out into the raging air. In that moment I saw the deep blueness shine forth like fluorescent light into the fine spray coming off his body.

POSTSCRIPT

A REFLECTION

My father was something of a relic from Old Japan. Paying little attention to our household affairs, he stormed through life with an unflagging intensity and a fierce aversion to compromising his own standards and principles. It is probably due to his example that I have had a highly competitive nature since I was a child.

Even playing the board game of Go, one of my favourite pastimes, I have never been able to suppress my competitiveness. Not only when I first learned the game but even after I had attained some proficiency (third rank), I would often call 'matta', 'wait!' to change my move. I simply hated to lose. Sometimes I would get annoyed with myself for being so absurdly focused on winning, but my distaste for losing was stronger.

At the same time, and I do not mean to sound pompous, success in many endeavours, including academic work, has always come fairly easily to me. I was awarded a cash prize in a sculpture exhibition and was always ahead of my peers in improving at sports.

Caught in the synergy between my abilities and my competitiveness I was afraid that, being fairly good at whatever I did, I would become a proverbial jack-of-all-trades but master of none. It struck me at such times that I faced a difficult challenge in trying to conquer myself.

From the time I was in elementary school I began to notice the warm family atmosphere of other people's homes. Such households impressed me as filled with a subtle mood of happiness that was very appealing. I was probably more sensitive to such simple domestic bliss than people who had been raised in close, affectionate home environments, where parents and children naturally spent a lot of time together. Thenceforward I came to suspect that happiness lies in the simple, unremarkable pleasures of ordinary, everyday life.

These childhood musings probably laid the groundwork for my philosophical contemplation in later years. I doubt that I would have become who I am today, armed with only the intelligence and competitiveness inherited from my father. On the other hand, I would hardly be qualified to talk about the urge to contribute if I had been the type who failed at everything he did. In short, I think it is precisely because my temperament naturally spans such a wide spectrum of sensibilities that I came to speculate on certain philosophical questions – the finiteness of human life, the idea of the urge to contribute, and so on – in my early teens. These are the themes of an ongoing study of human being that I regard as my life work, and this volume records one part of it.

REFERENCES

℞

Daskalova, Mariia Atanasova, and Khristo Danov. *Shosetsu Suparutakusu* [Spartacus]. Translated by Doi Masaoki and Matsunaga Rokuya. Sanseido, 1979.

Deeken, Alfons, and Iizuka Masayuki, eds. *Nihon no hosupisu to shumatsuki iryo* [Japanese Hospices and Terminal Healthcare]. Vol. 4 of *Sei to shi o kangaeru semina*. Shunjusha, 1991.

Drucker, Peter. *P. F. Dorakka keiei ronshu: Sudeni hajimatta 21 seiki* [Peter Drucker on the Profession of Management: The Twenty-first Century Already Begun]. Translated by Ueda Atsuo. Diamond Sha, 1998. (Drucker, Peter. *Peter Drucker on the Profession of Management.* Harvard Business School Press, 1998.)

Gaarder, Jostein. *Sofi no sekai* [Sophie's World]. Translated by Ikeda Kayoko and supervised by Suda Akira. Nippon Hoso Shuppan Kyokai, 1995.

Hirayama Ikuo. *Michi haruka* [The Road Afar]. Nihon Keizai Shimbunsha, 1991.

Kamei Katsuichiro, *Ai no mujo ni tsuite* [On the Transience of Love], Kodansha, 1971.

Kinoshita Reiko. *Obei kurabu shakai* [The Club]. Shinchosha, 1996.

Kono Shozo, ed. *Goingu konsan no keieigaku* [Management Studies on Going Concerns]. Zeimu Keiri Kyokai, 1996.

Murata Kiyoshi, ed. *Girishia bijutsu* [Greek Art]. Vol. 5 of *Taikei sekai no bijutsu*. Gakushu Kenkyu Sha, 1974

Nara Yasuaki. *Bukkyo no oshie* [The Teachings of Buddhism]. Vol. 1 of *Nihonjin no Bukkyo* (supervised by Nakamura Hajime). Tokyo Shoseki, 1983.

Shestov, Lev. *Shi no tetsugaku: Hakanaki mono no tetsugaku* [Philosophy of Death: Philosophy of the Evanescent]. Translated by Ueno Shuji. Yukonsha, 1971.

Shimazaki Toshiki. *Kanjo no sekai* [The World of the Emotions]. Iwanami Shoten, 1969.

Sonoda Tan. *'Mugen' no shii* [Speculation on "the Infinite"]. Sobunsha, 1987.

Taki Fujitaro Tsuisoroku Kanko Sewanin Kai (Committee for Publishing Memoirs about Taki Fujitaro), ed. *Ningen: Taki Fujitaro* [The Life and Ideas of Taki Fujitaro]. Nihon Kotsu Bunka Kyokai (Japan Traffic Culture Association), 1991.

Yamamuro Shizuka. *Girisha shinwa* [Greek Mythology]. Shakaishiso Sha, 1989.